Benjamin Keach

War with the Devil

Or the young man's conflict with the powers of darkness

Benjamin Keach

War with the Devil
Or the young man's conflict with the powers of darkness

ISBN/EAN: 9783337043063

Printed in Europe, USA, Canada, Australia, Japan

Cover: Foto ©Lupo / pixelio.de

More available books at **www.hansebooks.com**

WAR with the DEVIL:

OR THE

Young MAN's Conflict

WITH THE

POWERS of DARKNESS;

Displayed in a Poetical DIALOGUE between YOUTH and CONSCIENCE.

Wherein is set forth the Power of Corruption, and the Nature of true Conversion, in all its various progressive Steps.

Originally Written
By the late Rev. Mr. BENJAMIN KEACH.
Now revised and greatly improved
By Another. HAND.

Necessary to be read in all Christian Families.

Except a Man be born again, he cannot see the Kingdom of God, John iii. 3.

COVENTRY:
Printed by and for T. LUCKMAN.
AND SOLD BY
J. FULLER, in *Newgate-Street*, near *Cheapside*; J. JOHNSON, opposite the *Monument*, and S. CROWDER, in *Pater-noster-Row*, London.

(Price One Shilling bound.)

THE EDITOR's PREFACE.

Christian Reader,

*T*HIS Book hath gone through many Editions, since its first Appearance in the World; and I doubt not but it has been a chosen Shaft in the Quiver of the Almighty, and often hit the Joints of the Harness, and penetrated the Heart of the most obdurate Sinner.

For this Purpose it was well aimed when first published by the Reverend and Pious Author. But through Length of Time, and the Improvement of Language since then, the Style is now become somewhat obselete, and the Poetry lame. And as this may probably be the Cause why this excellent little Book is grown so scarce, and has been so long out of Print, the Editor deems his revising the Style, and correcting the Poetry, in order to render it more useful in the present Age, a sufficient Apology for attempting its Revival.

But it may be objected, There are many excellent Things of this Nature now extant, dress'd in modern Language, which seem to render this superfluous.

To which I answer, It is true, there are many excellent Things of modern Date, upon most Topicks of Divinity, yet none seems better calculated to do Good than this.

The

The Language is plain and familiar, easy to be understood, very instructive, and apt to draw the Attention; it may be read in a small Space of Time, purchased with a trifling Expence, and retained (at least the Sense and Relish of it) with little Burden of Memory.

It is likely to alarm the most stupid and secure Sinners, with a Sense of their extreme Danger; and to convince the superficial Professor and Formalist, of the Insufficiency of partial Reformation; nor is it less likely, to speak Consolation to those, who have sold all, to purchase the Pearl of great Price. Here they may look back with Pleasure, and trace the various Steps the Spirit of God hath taken, in convincing and converting them to himself; rescuing them from the fatal Snares and Allurements of the World, the Flesh, and the Devil; and making them Conquerors, and more than Conquerors, through him that loved them, and gave himself for them.

Here it may be proper to inform the Reader, that though the old Appendix, formerly annexed to this Book, viz. a long Dialogue between an old Apostate and a young Professor, is left out, as far less useful than the Body of the Work, yet he will find all that was truly excellent and valuable in former Editions preserved, improved, and rendered much more intelligible to every Capacity, than before; and though almost every Line be altered, yet the original Meaning of the Author is preserved as much as possible, and the Work rendered more generally instrumental, to promote the Glory of God, and the Good of Mankind: And if it may tend to bring about these salutary Ends, it will fully satisfy the Editor, whose Heart's Desire and Prayer is, that it may be accompanied with a divine Blessing unto every one, into whose Hands it may come.

WAR

WAR
WITH THE
DEVIL, &c.

YOUTH *in his* NATURAL STATE.

YOUTH.

THE Nat'ralifts, with Aptitude, compare
My Age to Spring's fweet Seafon of the Year,
When *Sol* falutes our Eyes, with Rays divine;
Approaching *Aries*, that celeftial Sign:
From whence he warms the Earth, and makes it bring
Forth Flow'rs and Fruits, and ev'ry pleafant Thing.
The Plants of ev'ry Kind, and op'ning Flow'rs,
Adorn the Meadows after trickling Show'rs.
The Lambs, forgetful of paft pinching Pain,
Skip now with Pleafure o'er the flow'ry Plain.
Behold, thofe Things that feem'd in Winter dead,
Spring forth afrefh, and brifkly fhew their Head;
Having obtain'd a joyful Refurrection,
By *Sol*'s bright chearing Beams, and warm Reflexion.

The Young Man's carnal Resolution.

Now, in the charming pleasant Month of *May*,
The Meadows wear their Cloathing, rich and gay:
The Earth adorn'd with Garments, red and green,
Purple and yellow, glorious to be seen.
The *Daisy*, *Cowslip*, *Violet*, and *Rose*
Glare in our Eyes, and Beauties rich disclose.
The chirping Birds, with their melodious Sounds,
Delight our Ears, and Pleasure all abounds.
The *Winter's* past; the *Storms*, the *Snow*, the *Rain*
Are now forgot, with ev'ry irksome Pain.
Nothing but Joy, and sweet Delights appear,
While lasts this flow'ry Season of the Year.
And thus it is with me in youthful Prime;
In Sports and Merriment I'll spend my Time:
As Birds of Pleasure frisk with easy Wing;
So, with my Fellows, I'll rejoice and sing.
I'll spend my Days in Pleasure, Mirth, and Joy;
Nothing on Earth shall e'er my Mind annoy:
For I'm resolv'd to range the World about,
And search and suck the Sweetness of it out.
No Stone I'll leave unturn'd, that I may find
New Scenes of Pleasure for my craving Mind.
The *Preacher's* Fancies shall not scar my Soul;
Fear shall be bury'd in a spacious Bowl.
At Cards and Dice, and such brave Games I'll play;
And like a Courtier dress me fine and gay:
With smart Bag-wig, lac'd Cloaths, gilt Sword and Cane
Amongst the sparkling Beaus I'll lead the Van.
With Dainties rich I'll feast my Appetite;
Nor once deny my Heart the least Delight.
I'll drink, and sport among the jov'al Crew,
Nor fear what Consequences may ensue;

I'll court the Fair; this Thing I likewise love,
Tho' I defign'dly fhall unconftant prove;
For this will tend to gratify my Senfe,
And make my Pleafure boundlefs and immenfe.
Whate'er my Ears would hear, mine Eyes behold,
Or Soul defire, fhall never be controul'd:
If all my Fortune will thofe Things procure,
I'll fpare no Coft fuch Pleafures to enfure.
Thus fhall my Life, with new Delights, be bleft,
Whilft others are with anxious Thoughts diftreft;
Whofe Minds, by ftrange Conceits, are fill'd with Pain,
Thinking, by lofing, all thereby to gain.
Such foolifh Riddles I could never learn;
Objects of Senfe are only my Concern.
Let fuch vain Fools their Minds with Fancies fill;
My Luft I'll gratify, and have my Will.
What State of Life can equal this of mine?
How far excelling what they call divine!
This is the prefent Purpofe of my Soul;
Who dares oppofe my Courfe, or me controul?

CONSCIENCE.

Controul thee, filly Worm! Yea, that dare I,
Since thou contemn'ft my juft Authority.
Thou tread'ft on me, without the leaft Regard,
As if I were not worthy to be heard.
Thou ftriv'ft to ftifle me, and down to Death
Wouldft me purfue, yet canft not ftop my Breath;
For ftill I'll haunt, and put thy Soul to Pain,
While thus my Sanction pure thou doft difdain.

Youth.

What! Who art thou that dar'ſt to be ſo bold?
I ſcorn to be by any Pow'r controul'd.
But now, I pray thee, tell; and let me know,
Whence comes thy Pow'r; come, thy Commiſſion ſhew.

Conscience.

Be not ſo hot, and thou ſhalt know my Name,
See my Commiſſion, alſo whence I came.
I'm no Uſurper; yet I thee command
Thy Courſe to ſtop, and make a preſent Stand.
Thy Pleaſures quit; break off thy vicious Courſe,
Or thou ſhalt feel a Hell of ſharp Remorſe.
Soon thou ſhalt ſee, and quickly thou ſhalt hear,
Such Things as ſhall affright thine Eye and Ear.
For all thy Courage, ere I thee forſake,
I'll bring thee News, enough to make thee quake.

Youth.

Whoe'er thou art, I'll make thee by and by,
Confeſs thou haſt accus'd me wrongfully:
From Murder I am clear; in Thought and Deed,
Therefore thy Charge recant; and pray, take heed.
But firſt of all, pray let me know thy Name;
Or hence depart, and hide thy Head for Shame.
Thou ſeem'ſt a quarrelſome Uſurper bold;
Yet know, by thee I'm not to be controul'd:
But ere thou go'ſt, thy Name declare to me,
Or I'm reſolv'd to be aveng'd on thee.

Conscience.

Have I accus'd thee wrongfully? ah, no!
I'll plainly prove my Charge before I go.
What greater Violence canst thou do more
Than thou hast done, and threaten'd me before?
Forbear thy Threats; be still, and hold thy Hand,
And thou my Name shalt quickly understand.
Yea, thou shalt know my Office, Pow'r, and Place
Of Residence; which Things may work out Peace.
I am Vicegerent to a mighty King,
Whose sov'reign Sway o'er-ruleth ev'ry Thing.
He keeps one Court above, and one below,
O'er which I'm Deputy, as thou shalt know,
To act and judge, according to my Light;
Impartially I give each Man his Right.
Those I condemn, who wilful Rebels are,
And justify th' obedient and sincere.
I'm charg'd to keep a Watch continually,
O'er all Men's Actions, with a careful Eye;
And therefore thee I likewise must accuse
Of many horrid Crimes, and sad Abuse
Of Time and Talents, which to thee were lent;
All which thou hast most shamefully mispent.
Nay, Murder, Treason, and such Villainy
Against the Crown and royal Dignity
Of that great Prince, from whom thou hast thy breath,
Thou hast committed, and incens'd his Wrath.
And I, the Deputy of this great King,
A Warrant have, thy guilty Soul to bring
Before his Bar, that thou may'st there confess
Thy horrid Crimes, and loathsome Wickedness.

A black

A black Indictment, I've drawn up in truth,
Against thyself, poor miserable Youth!
Thy Pride and Pleasure now I'll sadly mar,
Whilst thou standst trembling at thy Maker's Bar.
Thy sports and Games, and youthful Lusts shall be
No more a sweet and pleasing Scene to thee.
Thy Crimes forgot will all against thee rise,
And fill thy Soul with Terror and Surprize.
And now, to put thee also out of Doubt,
My Name is *Conscience*, which thou bear'st about:
I am that secret Monitor within,
Which in thy Breast beholds and checks thy Sins.
Truth is my Rule; Men's Courses I compare
According as their Minds enlighten'd are:
And when they walk contrary to that Light,
I then accuse them in their Maker's Sight:
But when their Talents they discreetly use,
I then their frail Infirmities excuse.
But thou hast walk'd, without the least Controul,
Against God's *Law*, and sinn'd against thy Soul;
Lo! thou art try'd, cast, and condemn'd by me,
Involv'd in Guilt, black Shame, and Misery.

YOUTH.

Conscience art thou? why art thou come so late?
Thy Admonitions now are out of Date.
Thou melancholy Ghost, away from me;
My Pleasure I'll pursue, in spite of thee.
Far better Guests, behold, to me are come;
Conscience, depart; for thee I have no Room.
Shall I be check'd by thee, a silly Thought?
And into Fear by foolish Fancy brought?

What!

What! was it thee that my Indictment drew?
Charg'd me with Treason, and with Murder too?
A Fig for thee, and all that thou canst do!
Forbear against me thus to prate and preach;
For I'm resolv'd at length thy Neck to stretch.
I'll swear, carouse, and play with Whores at Will,
Until I've stifl'd thee, and made thee still.
I'll clip thy Wings; and let thee see at length
I'm Over-match for thee and all thy Strength;
And if thou speak'st, I will not lend an Ear;
But turn my Back upon thee with a Sneer.
If thou grow'st noisy, when I'm all alone,
I'll haste away, and presently be gone
To those brave Boys, who toss the Pot about;
And thus, in Time, I'll tire thy Patience out.
To Plays and Masquerades, and Games sublime,
I'll go, and thus get rid of thee in Time.

CONSCIENCE.

Ah! stubborn, foolish Youth, be not so rash;
Or thou shalt quickly feel my cutting Lash.
I have a fearful Whip, and bitter Sting;
Soon will they make thee cease to boast and sing.
I'll gripe thee sore, and make thee howl and groan,
If thou in this mad Course of Sin go'st on.
As stubborn Necks as thine I've made to yield,
This shalt thou find before I quit the Field.
Go where thou wilt, thy wand'ring Feet I'll find,
And there torment and vex thy guilty Mind.
Nor is it in thy Pow'r to shake me off,
Tho' at me now thou seem'st to jeer and scoff.

Thou count'st me but a *Thought*, a fictious *Dream*;
But I'm commission'd by the King supreme,
To curb thy Course; nor will I fear thy Wrath,
Tho' thou hast threaten'd me with ling'ring Death.
I'll check thee daily in thy mad Career;
And this thy sinful Course shall cost thee dear.
The Fruits of Sin are certain Woe and Pain;
Cease then from Sin, if thou wouldst Peace obtain.
Since Light from Heav'n is darted into me,
While Sin remains, Disturbance thou must see:
Therefore let me advise thee as a Friend;
Refrain thy Course, and to my Voice attend:
Submit thyself to my Authority,
Which I've receiv'd from the great King most high.
If thou wouldst Peace and Pleasure here obtain,
No more my Counsel haughtily disdain;
But hear my Voice for once, be wise and try
Th' Experiment; then, if thou canst deny,
That my Advice is wholesome, then forbear
To hearken to my Voice, or yield to Fear:
If Pleasure is thy Choice, forsake thy Sin;
For no true Pleasure can be found therein:
But if thou wilt incline thine Ear to me,
If I do not more Joy afford to thee
Than all thy Sins; then ne'er believe me more,
But slight me still, as thou hast done before.
Consider well; what Comfort is in Sin?
What outward Peace, while there is War within?
'Tis all a Cheat to hope for Pleasure here,
Unless thou dost thy sinful Course forbear:
Get Peace within; but that thou ne'er canst do,
Until thou bidd'st thy vain Delights adieu.

This

Conscience *reasoning with* Youth.

This will, if once obtain'd, afford more Joy
To thy poor Soul, than all thy Gold will buy.
  And now, since we're alone, let thee and I
More midly talk about Supremacy.
  Will it be best to let *Corruption* reign,
Which nought procures but Sorrow, Shame, and Pain,
And *Conscience* to reject, whose Love to thee,
From Bondage, Sin and Shame, would set thee free?
Have not these rampant Lusts, that rule the Sense,
Brought many Men to Shame and Indigence?
What brave Estates have some consum'd thereby,
And now are glad in Barns on Straw to lie?
How many Families have been undone,
By walking in that Way thou hast begun?
How many swagg'ring Sparks have thus been brought
To stinking Goals, where they must pine and rot?
How many swing at *Tyburn* ev'ry Year,
For their neglecting my Advice to hear?
Yea, many Thousands have been quite undone,
While they my wholesome Counsels strove to shun.
Some stop my Mouth a Time; I cannot speak,
And then they sport and play, and merry make,
Thinking I'm dead, and ne'er shall gripe them more,
But with keen Lashes soon I make them roar.
Nay, some of them I drive into Despair,
When in their Faces I begin to stare;
Nor Peace by Night or Day their Spirits find,
I so perplex and haunt their troubled Mind.
What say'st thou now, poor *Youth*?—Wilt thou submit?
Weigh well the Danger, and the Benefit.
Thou seest the Danger is immensely great,
If Men rebel, and *Conscience* ill intreat.

Nor is their Profit lefs, who, Heart and Hand,
Freely submit themselves to my Command.
Now what say'st thou? Wilt thou my Voice obey?
Or wilt thou walk in the forbidden Way?

YOUTH.

Was ever *Youth* perplex'd and tofs'd as I,
Who flourish'd fair in my Prosperity?
Conscience, like some foul Fiend, dogs me about:
Where'er I go, within Doors or without:
At Home, abroad, by Night or Day, I find
No Rest nor Quiet for my tortur'd Mind.
Conscience, what is the Cause thou mak'st such Strife
I can't enjoy the Comforts of my Life.
I am so grip'd and pinch'd within my Breast,
I know not where to go, nor where to rest.

CONSCIENCE.

The Cause is plain, thou need'st not ask me why
Thou know'st, my Sanction thou wouldst not obey:
Thou hast not walk'd according to thy Light;
But wilful sinn'd with all thy Mind and Might.
I am God's faithful Witnefs, and must speak
Whene'er thou dost his righteous Precepts break.
This is the Office he hath fixt me in,
To warn, exhort, and reprimand thy Sin.
I must reprove, and sharply thee accuse,
While thus thy Maker's Gifts thou doth abuse.
I can't betray my Trust, nor hold my Peace,
Until thou dost thy vicious Courses cease:
'Till thou thy dear beloved Lusts forsake,
I shall pursue, and make thy Heart-strings ach.

YOUTH.

Conscience, forbear, and keep thy sage Advice;
I can't conform, thy Rules are too precise.
Knock at my Door no more; I tell thee plain,
Thy Admonitions wholly I disdain.
Lo, I'm a Man of Fortune, brave and gay,
I cannot stoop to such a low-liv'd Way;
'Tis much below my Birth and Parentage,
And it agrees not with my present Age.
Therefore forbear, I cannot now regard
This grave Advice I have so often heard.

CONSCIENCE.

Alas! proud Flesh, dost think thyself too high
To yield, and bow to God's Authority;
Whose Deputy I am, and thence derive
Pow'r to suppress the stoutest Man alive?
My Pow'r is great, and my Commission large;
There's not a Man but I with Folly charge:
The *King* and *Peasant* are alike to me,
I favour none of high or low Degree:
When they transgress, I in their Faces fly
Without Regard, or Fear of Standers-by.

YOUTH.

Forbear thy boasting; dost thou not perceive,
That scarce a Man or Woman will believe
One Word thou say'st, thou'rt grown so out of Date;
Be silent then, nor more presume to prate.
Thy Credit in the Country is but small;
There's few or none can thee abide at all.

The

The *Husbandman* his *Landmark* can't remove,
But straight thou dost him bitterly reprove;
Nor plow a Furrow of his Neighbour's Land,
But thou command'st him presently to stand;
There's not a Man can step the least awry,
But out against him fiercely thou dost fly;
The People ev'ry where thou dost so tire,
They've banish'd thee almost from ev'ry Shire;
And in the City thou art so abhorr'd,
There's very few will now believe thy Word;
For if they did, they could not, as they do,
Their various Paths of Pleasure so pursue;
Their Pride and Luxury, and gaudy Dress,
Their Swearing, Cheating, and their Drunkenness,
With many other Vices, would decay,
If they believ'd the Things that thou dost say.
The Whores and Bawds, the Stews and Brothels then
Would be detested by all Sorts of Men;
The Stage would languish, and the Actors mourn,
Or change their Trade, and all their Play-books burn.
'Twould change the Face of Things, and quite destroy
The sweet Delights that People now enjoy;
'Twould make our swagg'ring *Beaus* their Heads hang
And airy *Youth* look like a Country Clown; [down,
Nay, half Fanatics we should quickly be,
If we believ'd and hearken'd much to thee:
But this one Thing revives and chears my Heart,
There's few in Town or Country takes thy Part,
Only a few, whom we wild Nicknames give;
Abhor'd by all, and judg'd not fit to live.
'Tis out of Fashion grown, all Men may see,
Conscience, to mind thee in the least Degree.

He

He that can't whore and swear, without Controul,
We count a foolish, weak, and tim'rous Soul:
Therefore, tho' thou so desp'rately dost fall
On me, poor *Youth*; yet lo! I hope I shall
Get loose from thee, and then I'll tear the Ground,
And in consummate Pleasure long abound.

CONSCIENCE.

Ah! poor deluded *Youth*, dost thou not know,
That most Men in the fatal broad Way go?
And what, tho' they against me thus rebel,
Wilt thou with them plunge headlong into Hell?
For all, who will of me no Warning take,
Are hast'ning down to that tremendous Lake.
And what, tho' I'm in no Request with them,
Don't they likewise the Word of God contemn?
Don't they the Law and Gospel both despise,
Lest these should from their *Idols* turn their Eyes?
And what, tho' such as do my Voice obey,
Are in the World despis'd, and made a Prey
To ev'ry rav'ning Wolf of savage Breed?
Yet doth their inward Peace abundantly exceed.
It far excels whate'er the World can give,
For they in true substantial Pleasures live.
Come then, proud soul, nor longer now contend,
But leave thy Lusts, and to my Sceptre bend;
For I'll not leave thee in this State secure,
But close pursue thee to thy dying Hour:
And if thou dost not with my Words comply,
I'll hang upon thee to Eternity;
And, like a deathless Viper, make thee smart,
With endless Gnawing at thy tortur'd Heart.

YOUTH.

YOUTH.

Conscience, forbear; for I'm resolv'd to fly
Where I may hide me from thy teazing Eye.
There I'll enjoy myself, exempt from Pain,
And thou to find me shall attempt in vain.

CONSCIENCE.

Ah! foolish *Youth*, think how can this be done!
From *Conscience* 'tis in vain to try to run:
No universal Place thou canst descry,
Will ever hide thee from my piercing Eye.
With equal Ease thro' Dark and Light I see;
No Cov'ring hides thy secret Crimes from me:
Where'er thou art, lo! I am always near,
To scar thy guilty Soul with tort'ring Fear.
Could *Cain* or *Judas* from my Presence fly,
Or hide their Crimes from my accusing Eye?
Did not I close pursue them to the End,
And make them rue their Madness, to offend
My glorious Prince, and me his true Viceroy?
How soon did I their flatt'ring Bliss destroy?
Oh! then, deluded *Youth*, I pray take heed,
Be well advis'd, if e'er thou wouldst be freed
From Veng'ance here, and endless Wrath to come,
When Death shall call thee hence to hear thy Doom.

YOUTH.

What! can I neither flee, nor thee subdue?
Conscience, I pray thee, do not then pursue!
Follow me not so close; forbear a-while;
Do not so soon my Youth and Beauty spoil!

Th

Youth *parleys with* Conscience; *but in vain.*

This is the Flow'r and Spring-tide of my Age,
Oh! pity me, and cease thy bitter Rage.
Crop not the tender Bud; 'tis yet too green;
How many pleasant Days have others seen?
Let me enjoy the same, nor on me frown;
Forbear thy Hand till my wild Oats are sown.
With others thou hast borne, Time after Time,
And wilt thou not grant me the flow'ry Prime
Of those good Days, which God on me bestows?
Oh! do not thou my just Request oppose.
And when I've spent my Youth in Gallantry,
Then I'll grow sage, and take Advice of thee.
Mean-time, let me my youthful Days employ
In what young Men esteem their chiefest Joy.

CONSCIENCE.

What! after all thy saucy Insults great,
Dost thou begin by Flatt'ry to intreat?
And think'st thou thus o'er *Conscience* to prevail?
Ah, vain Conceit! this Effort soon will fail.
'Tis quite against my Nature, know in truth,
To wink at Sin, or thus to pity Youth.
From God I no such Liberty derive;
Nor will I at the smallest Sin connive.
Did God in Wrath, blow me, thy Candle, out,
Then thou in Sin might'st quietly take thy Rout;
But woe to thee that ever thou wast born,
If from thy Soul the Light should thus be torn!
To grope in Darkness, wallowing in thy Sin;
Then will thy never-ending Woes begin.
But whilst in thee remains that legal Light,
Against thy Sins I cannot cease to fight.

S. They're odious in God's Sight; nor will he give
One Moment's Liberty in Sin to live.
Great is thy Danger, if thou doſt delay,
Or put off thy Repentance for a Day!
Whate'er thy Hand finds thee this Day to do,
With all thy Might immediately purſue *.
But if thou wilt not me believe, O *Youth!*
Go ſearch God's ſacred Oracles of Truth.

YOUTH.

Well, *Conſcience*, ſince no Peace thou wilt afford,
I'll then apply to God's ſure written Word.
So far I'll with thy Counſel now comply,
For I am ſorely troubled inwardly.
I'll make a Trial; I'm reſolv'd to ſee
If *Conſcience* and the Word of Truth agree.
Truth cannot err, nor lie, tho' *Conſcience* may;
For that miſguided often leads aſtray:
But if they both declare the ſelf-ſame Thing,
'Twill ſome Amazement to my Spirit bring.
Now my Requeſt, and all I humbly crave,
Is ſome ſhort Time in youthful Luſts to have.
Conſcience denies me this; *Truth*, what ſay'ſt thou,
Oh, pity me, and this ſmall Boon allow!
To me, poor Lad, alas! I am but young,
A tender Flow'r, that is but lately ſprung
From Nature's Soil; and *Conſcience* Day and Night
Harraſſes me with all his Main and Might.
Juſt as the Froſt the tender Bud deſtroys,
So doth he ſtrive to ſtop my early Joys.

* Eccl. ix. 10.

Must I reform, and all my Lusts forsake?
O then some fitter Season let me take!
For all Things under Heav'n, lo! there's a Time,
O let me then enjoy my youthful Prime!
When I'm grown older I'll return to God,
And shun the Path my youthful Feet have trod.

TRUTH.

Hold, hold, vain *Youth!* thou art mistaken now,
No Time to live in Sin doth God allow.
If I may speak, attend, and thou shalt hear;
For I with *Conscience* also Witness bear:
I am his Guide, his Rule, and by my Light
He acts, dictates, and speaks the Thing that's right:
Therefore thou art undone, if thou deny
To hear his Voice, and with his Words comply.
Art thou too young thy sinful Ways to leave?
And hast thou not a precious Soul to save?
Art thou too young to leave thy Vanity,
When old enough for it in Hell to lie?
Some fitter Season, *Youth,* dost think to find?
'Tis Satan this suggests into thy Mind.
A fitter Season never can be found,
Than when God calls; and now thou hear'st the Sound,
" Return to me, return now speedily,
" Why wilt thou thus reject my Voice and die *?"
Those who rebellious are to his sweet Voice,
Shall one Day rue their mad delusive Choice.
But, *Youth,* pray once more lend an Ear to me,
Whilst thou art young thy Maker calls to thee,

* Ezek. xxxiii. 11.

" Remember

" Remember thy Creator in thy Youth *."
Now, now obey the Voice of sacred Truth.
The first ripe Fruits of old the Lord requir'd †,
And still of thee the same is yet desir'd,
That thou to him a Sacrifice should give
Of thy best Days ‡, and learn betimes to live
Unto the Praise of his most holy Name;
And not by Sin his Glory to blaspheme.
This is, dear *Youth*, thy happy chusing Time,
While thou dost flourish in thy youthful Prime.
" Set thy Affections on the Things above §,"
And seek an Int'rest in the Saviour's Love.
Did not Jehovah first thy Breath bestow,
And also place thee on this Earth below?
And many precious Blessings to thee give,
That thou to him alone shouldst subject live?
Think how he sent his own beloved Son,
To die for Crimes, that rebel Worms had done.
Behold him nail'd to an accursed Tree,
For Crimes committed by such Foes as thee:
But whilst in wilful Sin thou dost remain,
Thou striv'st him still to crucify again ‖.
Thy crimson Sins are odious to the Lord,
Or he had never drawn his dreadful Sword,
And sheath'd it in the Bowels of his Son,
To satisfy for what such Crimes had done.
Nothing appears more hateful in his Sight
Than these base Lusts in which thou tak'st Delight ╪.

* Eccl. xii. 1.   † Exod. xxii. 29.
‡ Eccl. xi. 9.   § Col. iii. 2.
‖ Heb. vi. 6.   ╪ 2 Pet. ii. 10.

And wilt thou not, vain *Youth*, be yet deterr'd
From thy vain Ways? What! is thy Heart so hard
That nothing yet will cause it to relent,
And of thy num'rous Follies to repent?
Give Ear to *Truth*, *Truth* never told a Lie,
" Flee youthful Lusts *," that dang'rous Vanity,
And now obey thy Maker's gracious Call
To seek his heav'nly Kingdom first of all,
And all Things needful then shall added be;
Nothing that's good shall be witheld from thee †:
But if thou dost this golden Time neglect,
And this his Call and Promises reject,
Unmindful of the Things that do pertain
Unto thy Peace and everlasting Gain,
Then God provok'd will wait on thee no more,
But shut against thee Mercy's open Door,
And leave thee howling at the golden Gate,
Crying for Entrance when it is too late.
While Terms of Peace thy Maker doth afford,
Yield to his Call, lest he unsheath his Sword;
For if his dreadful Wrath thou dost provoke,
He'll break thy Bones with an eternal Stroke ‡.
Who can before his Indignation stand?
Or bear the Weight of his uplifted Hand?
Let earthy Potsheards with each other jar,
But who dare with their Maker wage a War §?
Wilt thou with Satan, his grand Foe, combine,
And say o'er thee Christ Jesus shall not reign?
Wilt thou, vile Traytor-like, contrive the Death
Of that great King from whom thou hast thy Breath?

* 1 Pet. ii. 11.   † Mat. vii. 7.
‡ Psal. ii. 9.   § Isa. xlv. 9.

Wilt thou caſt Dirt upon the Holy One,
And keep *Immanuel* from his rightful Throne?
Over thy *Conſcience* 'tis his Right to ſway *;
Dar'ſt thou oppoſe his Reign, and diſobey?
Wilt thou reſiſt his dread and ſov'reign Pow'r?
Or dare to parley with him for an Hour?
Or gratify the Devil, who thereby
Regains freſh Strength, his Throne to fortify
In thy proud Heart; and make his Kingdom ſtrong,
By tempting thee to ſin whilſt thou art young?
But here the Word of God again breaks in:
" As well may *Æthiopians* change their Skin,
" Or Leopards purge the Spots that Nature gave,
" As old Tranſgreſſors their vile Cuſtoms leave †."
Dar'ſt thou, frail Worm, *Chriſt*'s Government oppoſe,
And with the Devil and Corruption cloſe?
A Slave to *Satan* hadſt thou rather be
Than take *Chriſt*'s eaſy Yoke, and be made free?
Which will afford moſt Comfort in the End,
The Lord to pleaſe, and *Satan* to offend;
Or *Satan* to obey, and ſo thereby
Declare thyſelf JEHOVAH's Enemy?
For whoſo lives in Sin, it is moſt clear,
That open Enemies to God they are.
And wilt thou yield unto the Devil ſtill,
And greedily obey his curſed Will?
Doſt think, vain *Youth*, that he will prove thy Friend,
When thou haſt drudg'd and ſerv'd him to the End?
Doth Sin (which is the Excrement of Hell)
Afford thy Noſe a ſweet and fragrant Smell?

---

* Rom. xiii. 5.   † Jer. xiii. 23.

And

And is *Chriſt Jeſus*, Source of all Delight,
Leſs worthy, and leſs lovely in thy Sight?
Wilt thou his Beauties, infinitely fair,
With Sin (the loathſom'ſt Thing on Earth) compare?
And ſhall thy Luſts be more eſteem'd by thee
Than all the Glories of th' eternal Three?
For that which Men do moſt eſteem they chuſe,
And Things of leſſer Value they refuſe.
But Chriſt (it ſeems) is nothing in thine Eyes,
Since thus thou doſt his Meſſages deſpiſe.
He calls, he knocks, and ſtill thou wilt not hear,
From his Reproofs thou turn'ſt away thine Ear.
Behold! he now ſtands knocking at thy Door,
With ev'ry good and precious Thing in Store:
Gold for the Poor, and Cloathing for the bare,
Food for the hungry, moſt exceeding rare.
The ſalutary'ſt Med'cines for Mankind,
Strength to the Lame, and Eye-ſalve for the Blind:
A Pardon for the Souls condemn'd to die,
And for poor Captives glorious Liberty.
All theſe he hath, and freely doth beſtow
(Without Reward) on thoſe that to him go:
Yea, all the richeſt Things of Heav'n above
He hath to give, yet nothing makes thee move
To ope' the Door; but ſtill he calls and knocks,
'Till wet with Dew are his moſt precious Locks;
And with the Drops of the long tedious Night
His Head is wet, while thou his Calls doſt ſlight;
And rather hugg'ſt thy Luſts and Pleaſures ſtill,
Than yield that Chriſt with Heav'n thy Soul ſhould fill:
Tho' he ten thouſand thouſand Worlds excels,
And makes the happy Soul, wherein he dwells,
         Enjoy

Enjoy a little Heav'n while here on Earth,
Filling it up with endless Joy and Mirth:
Which makes grey-headed Winter like the Spring,
And happy *Youths*, like heav'nly Angels, sing.
Such Souls he doth so highly elevate,
All earthly Phantoms they abominate;
And sensual Pleasures they no more compare,
With *Christ*, who is incomparably fair.
Nay, his Reproach, the Scandal of his Cross
They gladly bear, nor fear to suffer Loss:
Let me perswade thee then to taste and try
How good he is *; for then with boundless Joy,
Thou wilt admire the Beauties of his Face,
And matchless Riches of his glorious Grace;
That e'er thy happy Ears were blest to hear
Of such a Saviour, such a Saviour dear!
And that he deign'd to send thee such Advice,
To bring thy wand'ring Soul to Paradise,
When he had purchas'd (on th' accursed Tree,
With his own Blood) a Pardon dear for thee;
And, thy eternal Ruin to prevent,
Stoop'd down himself, and bore thy Punishment.
But none can know the Nature of that Peace,
And inward Joys he gives, which never cease,
But those few happy Souls who taste the same,
And are become the Follow'rs of the *Lamb*:
No Pen can set it forth, no Tongue declare,
Nor Heart conceive the Happiness they are
Possest of, who the Lord of Life enjoy,
Unfading Pleasures that will never cloy.

* Psal. xxxiv. 8.

Such is the Nature of Man's Heart and Breast,
He always pants for some substantial Rest.
But in his Search he finds all Vanity;
For nought on Earth his Soul can satisfy.
'Tis not in *Honour*, that's an empty Dream;
'Tis not in *Riches*, that is but the same;
'Tis not in carnal Pleasure, airy Mirth;
At last he owns it is not here on Earth:
For if to *Honour* swiftly he aspires,
Still, still he finds unsatisfy'd Desires.
Kingdoms and Crowns on tott'ring Bases stand,
The Servant soon the Master may command.
Belshazzar when upon his Throne of State,
How soon his Knees against each other beat!
How was he frighted, when, upon the Wall,
The mystic Letters soon foretold his Fall!
His impious Feast, and all his Pomp was vain,
Behold, that Night the boasting Mortal slain *!
Great Men are often fill'd with boding Fear,
And sore perplex'd, they know not how to steer.
Tall Cedars often fall, when Shrubs abide;
For Tempests blow, and strangely turn the Tide.
Man that's in Honour lives but little Space,
Dies like a Brute, so ends his mortal Race.
Where's *Nimrod* now, that mighty Man of old?
And where's the Glory of the Head of Gold?
Great Monarchs once, who golden Sceptres sway'd,
Are now ingloriously in Ruins laid.
The highest Place of human Government
Could never yield Ambition full Content;

* Dan. v. 5, 6, 30.

But

But if to *Riches* thou shouldst turn thine Eyes,
And think beneath that Stone the Pearl it lies,
Here thou wilt find a Disappointment still,
This World's not big enough thy Soul to fill.
If Store of Gold and Silver thou shouldst gain,
Riches increasing will increase thy Pain.
'Twixt Cares to get, and daily Fears of Loss,
'Twill more and more thy troubled Spirits toss.
Riches have Wings, and swift away they fly,
And leave their Owners in Extremity.
He that had Thousands by the Year last Night,
Is left as poor as *Job* by Morning Light.
Then, *Youth*, forbear on Wealth to set thy Mind,
For this of Bliss will leave thee far behind.
And if to *Pleasure* thou shouldst turn thine Eyes,
Thinking therein to find the mighty Prize,
This also will a Disappointment bring,
And cause thee mourn more than it made thee sing:
This airy God will but a Moment last,
And doleful Sadness follow it as fast.
Thy carnal Mirth, alas! how soon forgot?
Like crackling Thorns beneath a seething Pot.
And whilst thou striv'st thy sinful Lust to please,
Thy raging Conscience, *Youth*, who shall appease?
If sinful Pleasure seem like pleasant Meat,
The bitter Sauce thou wilt with Horror hate.
And as for *Beauty*, should it steal thy Heart,
Without the Beauty of the inward Part,
Lo, this will prove a most deceitful Snare,
And deep involve thee, ere thou art aware.
That *Beauty*, which Man's carnal Heart doth prize,
Is no more lovely in *Jehovah*'s Eyes,

Tho'

Tho' deck'd with Jewels, Rings, and rich Attire,
Than loathsome Swine that wallow in the Mire.
However fair, if yet defil'd with Sin,
They're but like painted Sepulchres within;
Nauseous and ugly in thy Maker's Sight,
Before whose Eyes Darkness is brought to Light.
  Besides, vain *Youth*, consider, by the Way,
How soon this outward *Beauty* will decay.
It fades and withers like the dying Grass,
Swift as the Shadows o'er the Meadows pass.
The curled Locks, and artful spotted Face,
Will soon be brought to Shame and foul Disgrace.
Those mincing Ladies, which in Pride excel,
Will soon be brought among the Worms to dwell;
Death and the Grave will soon their Pride controul,
And thro' their Cheeks the Worms will sweetly rowl.
None shall admire their sparkling Beauty more,
But ev'ry Eye the nauseous Sight abhor.
Nor will thine Age, of which thou seem'st to boast,
Avail thee long; thy Bloom will soon be lost:
Tho', like the Spring, thou seem'st to flourish gay,
Soon will thy flow'ry Season fade away.
  Or if on *Learning* thou shouldst set thy Mind,
And search 'till thou the deepest *Science* find;
Here thou wilt also find much Vanity,
Thy craving Soul 'twill never satisfy:
For all the human Learning here below,
Will never teach thee full thyself to know,
Much less inform thy fluctuating Mind
Where thou the Source of Happiness may'st find.
No; human Knowledge and Philosophy,
Can ne'er unfold the glorious Mystery

Of Godliness; God in the Flesh made known,
And now ascended to his Father's Throne.
What he hath done, and what he's doing now,
Is what concerns thy Happiness to know:
But, Oh! to know what Joys arise from hence,
Is what surpasses all the Pow'rs of Sense.
 Dote not on *Honour* then, nor earthly *Treasure*,
Beauty, nor *Learning*, *Youth*, nor carnal *Pleasure*.
All is but Vanity that lies below,
And all Earth's Glory but a gaudy Show.
Look then to Heav'n, and seek for higher Joys,
Let Swine take Husks, and Fools these earthly Toys.
Come thou to Christ, and of his sacred Rill
Of living Water, thou shalt drink thy Fill,
Which when thou tast'st, 'twill yield thee such Delight,
All earthly Joys will vanish out of Sight,
Unworthy of thy Notice any more,
When once possest of Christ's eternal Store;
For, lo! at his Right-Hand are endless Joys,
Infinitely surpassing earthly Toys.
And tho' on Earth his Saints such Troubles meet,
One Smile from him makes all their bitter sweet.
For in believing there's such Comfort plac'd,
When longing Souls the heav'nly Fatness taste,
That they esteem whate'er they meet below,
Unworthy of their Notice as they go,
From Strength to Strength, till they arrive above
At the blest Fountain of eternal Love.
Now if on Earth the Saints such Bliss obtain,
What shall they have when they in Glory reign?

YOUTH.

YOUTH.

Hold, hoary *Truth!* leave off, I cannot bear
Thy whining Strains; nor will I lend an Ear
To such wild Whims, such melancholy Stuff,
It suits not with mine Age; I have enough
Of it already, and enough of thee,
Since with my Int'rest thou dost not agree.
When I appeal'd to thee I was in Pain,
Tormented with a melancholy Strain;
But now the Cloud is broke, the Storm is o'er,
And thy Advice I think to ask no more.
Long-winded Sermons such as thine I hate;
Besides thy Doctrine now is out of Date.
I thought to have some longer Time to live
In Merriment, but none I find thou'lt give:
Therefore thy Counsel I disdain and spurn,
For mad Fanatic yet I will not turn,
Nor after such distracted People go,
For, lo! an easier Way to Heav'n I know.
My Lass, my Glass, my Sports and Company,
I'll yet enjoy in all my Bravery;
And I'll hold fast, yea, wantonly fulfil
My fleshly Mind, say Preachers what they will.
Therefore farewell, old *Truth*, I've done with thee,
Since thou deny'st my jov'al Liberty.

CONSCIENCE.

Ah *Youth!* ah *Youth!* and is it so indeed?
Wilt thou no more unto God's *Truth* give heed?
I now perceive 'twas but to stop my Mouth,
That thou dissemblingly appeal'dst to *Truth*.

But here, O *Youth*, thou may'ſt aſſured be,
What thou haſt heard has much enlighten'd me;
And my Commiſſion too, it doth renew,
As may appear by what will next enſue.
Haſt thou from God been called thus upon,
And is thy Heart ſtill harder than a Stone?
Thou canſt not now plead Ignorance, O *Youth!*
Thou'ſt heard thy Duty from the Word of *Truth:*
And this will grievouſly augment thy Sin,
If thou perſiſteſt wilfully therein.
Thy Guilt will be of deepeſt crimſon Dye,
And many Stripes will be procur'd thereby:
For whoſo knows his Maſter's Will, yet wide
From that known Path of Duty turns aſide,
His ſtubborn Back ſhall num'rous Stripes receive,
While he who knew not ſhall more Favour have.
Conſider this, O *Youth!* if thou refuſe
The Word of *Truth*, and *Conſcience* ſtill abuſe,
A ſturdy Rebel thou wilt prove to be,
For unto Chriſt thou wilt not bow the Knee.
Wilt thou retain thy Sins while thou doſt hear
How much againſt the righteous God they are?
And wilt thou ſpurn the Riches of his Grace?
Oh! tremble, Soul, at thy tremendous Caſe.

YOUTH.

Ah! now I ſee my pleaſant Days are o'er,
And youthful Sports I ſhall enjoy no more.
Conſcience, I find, will ne'er let me alone;
Alas, how ſoon my happy Days are gone!
Oh! that I could but ſin without Controul,
And *Conſcience* would no more diſturb my Soul;

Could I but have a little Respite giv'n,
Oh! that would be to me a little Heav'n.
But, ah! my *Conscience* is grown so severe,
His bitter Gripes I cann't much longer bear;
For he is grown so violent and strong,
I doubt my Fortress will not stand it long.
Such dreadful inward Conflicts now I feel,
My Courage sinks, and I begin to reel.
But yet I am resolv'd to try once more,
And struggle hard ere I the Fight give o'er;
I will not cowardly abscond the Field,
Nor at the first nor second Summons yield.
I'll make once more another stout Assay,
Ere I to *Conscience* will resign the Day.;
For how can I my sweet Delights forsake,
And not the stoutest Opposition make?
Conscience, altho' I sinful am, I see
There's many thousand Sinners worse than me.
There's none that lives, and from all Sin keeps clear,
This I from *Truth* did very lately hear.
And what tho' human Frailties oft beguile,
My Heart is good and upright all the while.

CONSCIENCE.

O mad deluded Wretch! dar'st thou commend
Thy rotten Heart, whence daily doth ascend
Such Clouds of inbred Lusts, which I behold,
Tho' hid from Men, 'twould shame thee were they told?
That base, polluted, vicious Heart of thine,
Is far more loathsome than a Stye of Swine:
There Vipers breed;. there hatch the Cockatrice;
There lies the Spawn of every hateful Vice.

'Tis like a painted Sepulchre within,
All full of Filth, and putrifying Sin;
Nay, out of it all Evil doth ascend,
And wilt thou yet thy filthy Heart commend?
And canst thou judge thy State yet good to be,
Because thou think'st there's many worse than thee?
Will that avail thee at the Judgment-Day,
When all the Wicked shall be swept away?
And thou amongst the rest, except thou turn,
Must sure with them in Hell for ever burn.
Without Repentance, *Truth* declares most plain,
All Men must perish in the burning Main †,
Where endless Flames of Brimstone round them rolls,
And there the deathless Worm torments their Souls ‡.

YOUTH.

Well, say no more; if it be so, I must
Appeal to *Truth* again, or I shall burst.
My troubl'd Heart will surely break, I see;
Therefore, O *Truth*, I must advise with thee.
What is my State, my Nature? tell me plain:
O sacred *Truth*, let me this Boon obtain!
I pray, explain this Thing to me more clear;
For *Conscience* scares me with uncommon Fear.
Doth he speak right, O *Truth*? or is he wrong?
For lo! I find Convictions in me strong.
What is my State, I pray declare to me;
And set my anxious Soul at Liberty?

TRUTH.

What *Conscience* speaks, believe me, *Youth*, 'tis right;
And thou in vain maintain'st the fruitless Fight *;

† Luke xiii. 5. ‡ Rev. xxi. 8. * Job. ix. 4.

For

For whilst against thee he doth Witness bear,
Thy real Danger plainly doth appear.
Those he condemns, by Light receiv'd from me,
Still under God's condemning Wrath must be;
For God is greater than thy Heart, O Soul,
And sees all thy Transgressions black and foul *.
If *Conscience* doth its Testimony give,
That thou in any sinful Course dost live,
And that thou'rt in an unconverted State;
And if from hence ariseth your Debate,
Great is thy Danger; canst thou this deny?
What wouldst thou do, if thou this Night shouldst die † ?
If in this dreadful State thy Life depart,
Undone for ever, O young Man, thou art!
As sure as God, the righteous God's in Heav'n,
Against thy Soul the Sentence will be giv'n.
Conscience from God alone his Pow'r derives ‡,
And whosoe'er against his Mission strives;
Rejecting his kind Motions, 'tis all one,
As if on Christ himself they tread upon.
While *Conscience* rules by Laws that are divine,
'Tis Treason him t'oppose or undermine.
And once more, plain to shew thee thy Estate,
Thou being young, and unregenerate;
No God, no Christ, no Heav'n hast thou §; ah! no,
This is the Cause and Sum of all thy Woe.
In God no Int'rest, *Youth*, thou hast at all;
He is departed ever since the Fall,
And is become a dreadful Enemy
To all the Workers of Iniquity.

* 1 John iii. 20.   † Prov. xii. 7.
‡ Rom. ii. 15.   § Eph. ii. 12.

The heavy Curses of his broken Law
Hang o'er thy Head; O Scene of dreadful Awe!
Ready with Vengeance on thy Soul to fall,
And crush thee down to everlasting Thrall.
Yea, all God's holy Attributes are met,
And all against thy guilty Soul are set,
To crush it with as great a Load of Woe,
As Pow'r can make a Creature undergo.
He'll fearfully thy Soul in Pieces tear;
And his eternal Veng'ance who can bear?
His Wrath will surely on thy Soul remain,
'Till thou by Faith art truly born again †.

YOUTH.

Ah! *Truth*, this Doctrine fills my Mind with Care
It is enough to drive one to Despair:
For, if 'tis so; I grant, I am undone:
But God is gracious, and hath sent his Son.
Full of Compassion is he, therefore I
Hope he'll on me his Mercy magnify.

TRUTH.

'Tis true, the Lord is gracious; yet will he
Not quit the Fearless, nor the Guilty free.
Gracious he is; yet is he full of Ire,
To wilful Sinners a confuming Fire *.
He sent his Son, indeed, for such to die,
Who do by Faith to him for Refuge fly.
But many falsly apprehend the Case,
And wantonly abuse his rich free Grace ‡;

† John iii. 36.   * Heb. xii. 29.   ‡ Jud. v. 4.

Whil

While, unconverted, they in Guilt remain,
Their Hope's delusive, and their Faith is vain:
Therefore, O *Youth*, my wholesome Counsel take,
Beware, lest thou an Application make
Of God's rich Mercy, and a Saviour's Blood,
Till thou hast well the Gospel understood.
Those that are whole need no Physician have,
None but diseased Souls Christ came to save *.
What judgest thou thy present State to be?
How stands the Matter 'twixt the Lord and thee?

YOUTH.

I am a Sinner: Oh! my Heart now bleeds;
My Sin-sick Soul a mighty Saviour needs:
My Conscience tells me I'm undone and lost;
And for my Sins my Soul is sorely tost.

TRUTH.

O *Youth*, no Saviour will asswage thy Grief,
Till thou art willing to receive Relief †.
For thy deep Wounds no Healing can there be,
Until the Cause of this thy Misery,
That sinful Cause, which brings such deadly Smart,
Be wholly rooted from thy carnal Heart ‡.

YOUTH.

My trembling Soul is now alarm'd with Fear;
Another Way, O *Truth!* my Course I'll steer:
All sinful Ways I must forsake; I see,
For these bring on me all this Misery.

* Matt ix. 12.   † John v. 40.   ‡ Isa. lix. 2.

I see what dreadful Danger I am in,
While I retain, and hug my darling Sin.
There's scarce a Night now passes o'er my Head,
But I'm afraid to close mine Eyes in Bed;
Lest, ere I wake to see the Morning Light,
Mine Eyes be clos'd in everlasting Night;
Where's nought but Darkness, and the dismal Yell
Of scorched Devils in the Flames of Hell.
My *Conscience* therefore loudly tells me now,
I must bid all my former Lusts adieu:
My Lies and Fraud, and all unlawful Gain;
My Sports and Games, and ev'ry Thing that's vain;
Refrain the Plays in which I took Delight,
And change the Scene, to pray both Day and Night.
Conscience has overcome me with his Gripes,
And *Truth* comes after with his threaten'd Stripes.
The Wall's broke down, the old Man runs away,
And *Conscience* close pursues to cut and slay:
He threatens hard, that he'll no Quarter give,
And seems before him ev'ry Thing to drive.
Lust now to Corners dark is forc'd to fly,
Where it continues lurking privily,
Watching an Opportunity to get,
Once more on *Conscience* manfully to set:
For tho' at present it is far estrang'd,
It hopes on *Conscience* still to be reveng'd;
Because he threatens hard with Might and Main,
And says Corruption must and shall be slain.
I side with him, because I would have Peace;
But still 'tis doubtful when these Wars will cease.

DEVI

DEVIL.

What Pity 'tis thy Sun should set so soon,
Or be o'erclouded thus before 'tis Noon!
In the Horizon it but just appears,
Nor sooner shines, but it's eclips'd with Tears.
Shall Winter come before the Spring is past,
And all its Fruit be spoil'd with one sad Blast?
Shall that sweet Flow'r, which seems so bright and gay,
So quickly fade, and wither quite away?
What Pity 'tis, that such a *Youth* as thee
Should thus be taken in Captivity?
Hear not what *Conscience* says; for I'll maintain,
'Tis better far to hug thy Sins again.
Thy *Conscience*, *Youth*, thou hast too lately found,
How he hath smit thee with a deadly Wound.
Consider well, and be advis'd by me;
My Ways are best, as thou shalt quickly see:
I'll give thee Honour, Wealth, and pleasant Things,
Such as are priz'd by Noblemen and Kings.
Let not this Make-bate, with an angry Frown,
Throw all thy Glory and thy Pleasure down.
Let no strange Thoughts distress thy troubl'd Mind;
What Satisfaction canst thou hope to find,
But in such Things as are enjoy'd in Time?
'Tis I must raise thee to the Throne sublime.
The Hell thou fear'st may prove an empty Dream;
The Heav'n thou hop'st for, that may be the same.
But if thou won't believe, and be aware,
I'll raise up more that will their Witness bear
To what I say; therefore, old Man, awake,
Rouze speedily; thy Life lies at the Stake:

And

The Devil *rallying his Forces again.*

And, Miſtreſs Heart, ſtir up thy manly Will,
Is this a Seaſon for him to be ſtill?
If he to *Truth* and *Conſcience* once give Place,
Our Int'reſt will, you'll ſee, go down apace.
Judgment is almoſt gone, I ſee him yield;
And Courage too, I fear, will quit the Field.
Some Luſts are ſlain, and in their Blood they lie,
And others into Holes are forc'd to fly.
As for *Affection*, he retains his own,
Tho' *Conſcience* doth upon him ſternly frown.
Remembrance will unto him treach'rous prove,
If I his Thoughts from Sermons can remove.
I'll make his Mind run after temp'ral Things,
And make his Thoughts play on their carnal Strings:
Then he'll forget what he did lately hear,
And ſoon renounce his former Thoughts and Fear.
If I can pleaſe his ſenſual Appetite,
There's no great Fear of any ſudden Flight.
His Breaſt is tender, apt to entertain
The Sparks of Luſt, nor can he well refrain.
I'll blow them up, and kindle them anew,
And to Convictions ſoon he'll bid adieu.
New Objects I'll preſent before his Sight,
In which I'm ſure he'll greatly take Delight;
I have ſuch Hold of him, there's no great Doubt,
But I once more ſhall turn his Mind about.
His old *Companions* alſo I'll provoke
To give his Door again another Knock.
Their ſtrong Inticements he can hardly ſtand,
But ſoon he'll yield to them both Heart and Hand.

YOUTH

Youth's old Companions.

How do you do, Sir? What's the Cause that we
Can ne'er of late enjoy your Company?
It seems to us as if you were grown strange,
As if in you there were some sudden Change.

Youth.

I have not had an Opportunity:
Besides, on me some heavy Burdens lie,
Which press my Spirits with a heavy Load,
On which Account I cannot go abroad.

Companions.

I warr'nt ye, Sirs, 'tis Sin afflicts his Soul,
And he's just turning a fanatic Fool.
Come, come away; to *Age* such Care belongs;
To *Youth* brave Mirth, gay Jollity, and Songs.
Banish these gloomy Thoughts with Pipe and Pot;
Carouse and sing 'till they are quite forgot.
The lovely Strains of Music, Harp, and Lute,
Where Plays are acted, these thy Age will suit.
Come, go with us upon a brave Design,
The which will chear that drooping Heart of thine.
Come, gen'rous Soul, let thy ambitious Eye
Such foolish Dreams, and Fancies vain, defy:
Shall thy heroic Spirit thus give Place
To silly Dotage, to thy great Disgrace?

Youth.

'Tis true; for Sin I've felt such cutting Smart,
As hath almost asunder rent my Heart:

And if you had the least Respect for me,
You would not laugh at my Calamity:
For tho' I am to your Delights inclin'd,
They bring a dreadful Burden on my Mind;
So that I must, if you this Course pursue,
Bid you and all these vain Delights adieu.

NEIGHBOURS *Remarks*.

Fain would he yield to them, because he fears
They will torment him with their Scoffs and Jeers:
But soon his Head begins again to ach,
Because his *Conscience* doth on him awake;
And when he sins, it stings him in such Sort,
As puts a Period to his jovial Sport.
The Thoughts of Death, which Sickness doth presage,
Afflicts him so, he cannot bear the Rage,
And inward Gripes of his enlighten'd Breast;
Therefore he owns at last, he thinks it best
To yield to *Conscience*, whom he long refus'd,
And grievously with Insolence abus'd.

CONSCIENCE.

Ah! vain deluded Wretch, canst thou believe
That thou thy *Conscience* canst with Shews deceive?
Thou mak'st the World thy outward Dress admire,
While thou appear'st in Hypocrite's Attire.
Hast thou to *Truth* so often lent an Ear,
And dost thou yet to Satan thus adhere?
Thou hadst as good have kept thy first Estate,
As thus deceitfully prevaricate.
To *Truth* appeal, if God give Space and Room,
Ere I pronounce on thee thy final Doom.

YOUTH.

YOUTH.

Alas! I am a poor afflicted *Youth*;
Conscience condemns me; I appeal to *Truth*.

TRUTH.

If *Conscience* thee condemn, which sees in Part;
Remember, God is greater than thy Heart,
And knoweth all Things, tho' in Secresy *
Thou in thy Bosom hugg'st Iniquity.
Consider then, before it be too late,
The dreadful Danger of thy present State.
If thou these friendly Warnings dost refuse,
And thus by Folly thy Convictions lose,
Sad is thy State, and dang'rous is thy Case;
For then thou slight'st thy Maker's boundless Grace †.
One Thing is needful ‡; that, alone, is good;
To have thy Soul wash'd in the Saviour's Blood;
This Thing alone will stand thee then in Stead,
In thine Extremity and greatest Need.
Thy Soul is precious, and of greater Worth
Than all the Treasures of this spacious Earth:
For if thou couldst the mighty Fabric gain,
And all its Wealth and Pleasures here obtain,
And in Exchange thy precious Soul shouldst lose,
Consider, Man, which Portion thou wouldst chuse §.
When once thy Soul is lost, thou losest all;
Then down to Hell must be thy final Fall;
And thou must know, what I of Hell declare,
And hid'ous Howlings of the Damned there.

* 1 John iii. 20.   † Prov. i. 24, 33.
‡ Luke x. 42.   § Matt. xvi. 26.

Ah! who with everlasting Flames can dwell?
Ah! who can bear the quenchless Fire of Hell *?
But this must all who in their Sins shall die;
This is their Portion to Eternity †.
Th' Unclean, the Drunkard, and the noxious Liar,
Must have their Part in that deep Lake of Fire:
With Thieves and Murderers of ev'ry Sort,
And Boasters proud, who at Religion sport.
Idolaters, Extortioners, and all
Who on the Rock of Avarice shall fall;
With all the vicious hypocritic Race,
And vile Apostates, Tramplers on rich Grace:
Let all such Sinners to my Words give Heed,
Their Torments will all human Thought exceed.
O then what wilt thou do? where canst thou fly,
To hide thyself from that dread Majesty,
Who tries the Reins, and searches ev'ry Heart,
And *Conscience* loud declares thou guilty art?
Wretch, lost and self-condemn'd, what canst thou do?
Lo! Justice at thy Heels doth close pursue.
As sure as God is true, if thou shouldst die
In that sad State, to all Eternity
Thou must in Hell's relentless Torments lie;
Except Repentance in thy Soul be wrought,
With dreadful Vengeance there thou must be brought.
Thy present Character doth plain declare
Thou art the Man, for whom God did prepare
That dreadful *Tophet* where the Damned are;
Which he hath made exceeding large and deep,
Such Wretches in that doleful Place to keep ‡.

* Isa. xxxiii. 14.   † Rev. xxi. 8.   ‡ Isa. xxx. 33.

Now

Now call to Mind what *Conscience* doth this Day
Charge thee withal, ere thou art swept away;
Lest thou from him shouldst hear no more at all,
Till thou into those quenchless Flames must fall:
What Mercy 'tis, that *Conscience* strives so long,
And his Convictions still in thee are strong:
O! fear, lest Sin should sear thy *Conscience* quite,
And God in Wrath put out thy Candle-Light,
And give thee up unto an Heart of Stone,
As he by many hath most justly done *.
Then canst thou not repent; 'twill be too late;
Such is the Danger of a lapsed State.

Youth, then no more this needful Work delay;
Nor dare to put it off another Day.
Thine own Experience must discover this,
Man's Life a Bubble and a Vapor is.
Thy Days on Earth, thou know'st, can be but few;
They fly away like Clouds of Morning Dew.
Thine Age unto the Spring thou dost compare,
And to the Flow'rs that then appear so fair:
From hence, O *Youth*, an useful Lesson learn,
Which may remind thee of thy great Concern.
The Grass that stands so thick, so green and gay,
Is soon cut down, and withers into Hay †.
So fly thy Days, thy golden Months, and Years,
Like that rich Lustre which so fair appears:
But on a sudden, lo! the Sun's bright Ray
Makes them recline their Heads, and fade away,
Like *Jonah*'s Gourd, which sprung up in a Night,
And dy'd as soon as it beheld the Light:

* Rom. i. 28, 29.   † Isa. xl. 6, 7.

Youth *promises to amend.*

Or like a swift-wing'd Ship with wide-spread Sail,
When she is driven by a mighty Gale:
Or like a Post, whose Haste the Sun outvies,
Or Weaver's Shuttle, which the Wind o'erflies *.
Now, *Youth*, beware, and measure not the Length
Of thy short Life by Vigour, Health, or Strength;
For these will all prove vain fallacious Rules,
Such as were never learnt in Wisdom's Schools.
Go to the Church-Yard, where dead Bodies lie,
There Graves of ev'ry Size thou may'st descry;
Which shew how short and frail is human Life,
How vain and fruitless all our Care and Strife.
Some think to live till far advanc'd in Age,
As did their Fathers ere they left the Stage;
But that is sure a most uncertain Rule,
Which oft deceives the poor unthinking Fool.
Thou hear'st the Things which thou shouldst reckon by,
Are of the swiftest Motion that doth fly;
Thy Days are on the Wing, they fly in Haste:
Few are thy Sands; they ev'ry Moment waste.
Of Dust thou art, to Dust thou must return;
And Judgment thou canst not one Day adjourn.
If now to Sin thou dost not learn to die,
Thy dreadful Ruin, *Youth*, is very nigh.
Consider then, and weigh within thy Mind,
What is thy Purpose? How art thou inclin'd?

YOUTH.

Thy Counsel, *Truth*, I am resolv'd to take,
And never more will I thy Ways forsake.

* See Job ix. 25. vii. 6.

I tremble

Youth's Hypocrisy discovered.

I tremble at the Thoughts of Death and Hell,
My Soul is wounded, and my Ulcers swell.
My Pains are great, and daily they increase ;
Therefore I am resolv'd to turn my Face
To Jesus Christ, that I may now obtain
Some healing Balsam to remove my Pain.
No rest can I, but in my Duty, find,
And now to Pray'r my Heart is much inclin'd ;
God will, I hope, my former Sins forgive,
Since I intend more godly now to live.
I'm now resolv'd to watch, and take such Care,
That Satan shall no more my Soul ensnare.

Neighbours *Observations*.

The *Youth* is now become a great Professor,
Though far from being yet a true Possessor
Of Christ's good Spirit, which if any lack,
He will not own, but on them turn his back.
Christ he has got into his Mouth and Head,
But is not risen with him from the Dead ;
But in old *Adam* still does he remain,
Not knowing ought of being born again.
When Satan sees, it is in vain to strive,
The Soul into its former Course to drive ;
But that it will gross Wickedness forsake,
And also will a fair Profession make ;
He yields thereto, resolving secretly,
To blind the Soul with close Hypocrisy ;
Knowing that such a splendid fair Disguise,
Is no less odious in JEHOVAH's Eyes.
New Avenues in Subtilty he finds,
To enter in, and cheat deluded Minds.

Them he perfuades, the War that's fought within,
Has overcome the mighty Powers of Sin.
The *Youth* now thinks his legal Reformation,
Is nothing lefs than real Renovation.
Here he fits down, and refts himfelf at Eafe,
When all is done, his *Confcience* to appeafe:
But now give Place to this religious Youth,
And hear a Dialogue 'twixt him and Truth.

YOUTH.

Happy am I, and bleffed be the Day,
When firft to *Truth*, and *Confcience*, I gave Way.
I would not be in my old State again,
If I thereby fome thoufands could obtain.
From Wrath and Hell my Soul is now fet free,
For I doubt not, Converfion's wrought in me,
The Word to me has with fuch-Pow'r been brought,
A glorious Change within my Soul is wrought.

TRUTH.

Ah! *Youth*, take Heed, left thou miftaken be;
Converfion is a Work moft rare to fee;
And very few that narrow Paffage tread,
While many Thoufands are miftaken led *:
They fall far fhort, for all their Strife and Pain,
Becaufe they ne'er were truly born again.
Come, let me hear the Grounds of thy Defence,
Since thou appear'ft fo full of Confidence:
I doubt thou ftill art underneath God's Curfe;
Then is thy State as bad, nay truly worfe

* Matt. vii. 13, 14.

Than

Truth *examines him further.*

Than 'twas when thou didſt no Profeſſion make,
But didſt thy Swing in all Profaneneſs take.
The *Phariſee* was a religious Man ;
Yet nearer Heav'n was the poor *Publican* *.
Conſider then, if ſhort of Chriſt thou cloſe,
Thou art undone ! conſign'd to endleſs Woes.

YOUTH.

What mean'ſt thou, *Truth ?* thou count'ſt my Words
But all may ſee that I converted am :   [a Flam;
But if my Grounds thou art reſolv'd to weigh,
Then pray give Ear to what I have to ſay.
The firſt fair Proof which I can freely bring,
To evidence and prove the real Thing,
Is the Convictions I have had of Sin,
Which once I hugg'd, and much delighted in.

TRUTH.

Alas ! poor Soul, this Proof will never bear ;
For moſt Men ſee, and own they Sinners are :
They are convinc'd likewiſe by inward Light,
That Sin is odious in their Maker's Sight :
Yet are they ſtill vile Sinners ne'ertheleſs,
And not one Dram of ſaving Grace poſſeſs.
King *Pharaoh, Eſau,* yea, and *Judas* too †,
Were all convicted of their Sin 'tis true ;
But that they were converted none believe,
For all theſe three the Devil did deceive.
And as he them beguil'd, ſo may he thee,
And deep involve thy Soul in Miſery ;

* Luke xviii. 14.
† Exod. x. 16, 17. Heb. xii. 16, 17. ' Matt. xxvii. 3, 4.

Nay,

Nay, this he has already I am sure,
Unless some better Proof thou canst procure,
To prove that thou indeed converted art,
And that thou hast obtain'd a pure new Heart,
Wrought by the Spirit of eternal Love,
Who only can the stony Heart remove.
There's many Men under Convictions lie,
And long remain, yet unconverted die.
Consider then what more thou canst produce,
For slight Convictions are of little Use.

YOUTH.

I do not only see my Sins, but I
Do therefore mourn and grieve continually:
And those that mourn for Sin they blessed are,
Don't *Truth* itself the very same declare *?

TRUTH.

Nay, don't mistake, for thou may'st weep amain,
And yet in thee Corruption still may reign.
Yea, thou may'st mourn for Sin, as many do,
For Fear of Shame, and sharp Remorse, and Woe,
Which Sin procures, and leads to in the End,
And not because their Maker they offend:
Nay, nor because they thus ungratefully
The Saviour strive afresh to crucify.
'Tis not the Evil that there is in Sin,
But the great Danger they descry therein:
This makes them tremble, grieve, lament, and mourn,
Lest they for it in Hell should ever burn.

* Matt. v. 4.

This Ground is weak; for *Esau*, it appears,
Thus mourn'd for Sin, with many bitter Tears *,
And yet 'tis sure that *Esau* was profane,
And far was he from being born again.

YOUTH.

But I go farther yet; for I confess
My horrid Crimes; and shameful Wickedness;
Which if I do, as I have often done,
The Lord is just; he is the faithful one,
Who will, as he hath said, pardon outright,
And blot my Sins intirely from his Sight †.
This being so, what Reason canst thou see,
Or whence alledge such dubious Thoughts of me?

TRUTH.

Ah! this won't do; 'tis not a certain Ground;
Many confess their Sins with Hearts unsound.
When *Pharaoh* saw the Judgments of the Hail,
His Heart began surprisingly to fail:
" I've sinn'd (said he) against the Lord most just;
" I and my People both are sinful Dust ‡!"
So *Saul*, and *Judas* likewise, both of them
Confess'd their Sins, yet God did them condemn.
Tho' each of these, when under Fear, exprest,
" Lord, we have sinn'd!" when *Conscience* them distrest.
Guilt glaring in their Faces, made them quake;
Then they, reluctant, forc'd Confessions make.
But such Confessions may be made in Pact,
Yet not of ev'ry Sin lodg'd in the Heart.

* Heb. xii. 16, 17.   † 1 John i. 9.   ‡ Exod. ix. 27, 28.

Men may confefs their Crimes, and own their Guilt,
Who yet Sin's horrid Nature never felt:
They may acknowledge in Extremity
Their glaring Faults, *Confcience* to pacify.
Thus may they do that they may Pardon crave,
Yet not defign thefe dear-lov'd Lufts to leave *.

Youth.

But I confefs not only, but forfake,
Therefore my State thou furely doft miftake.
Thofe who confefs their Sins, and leave them too,
God furely will to fuch his Mercy fhew.
Then trouble me no more; for, lo! 'tis plain,
I for my Part am truly born again.

Truth.

Ah! *Youth*, take heed, left thou deceiv'd fhouldft be,
Men may forfake all grofs Iniquity;
Yet in their Hearts fome Morfel fweet may lie,
Which they in Secret hug moft eagerly.
Sin they may leave, but not becaufe 'tis Sin,
As oftentimes has manifefted been.
If any Sin thou didft forfake aright,
All Sin would then be odious in thy Sight.
Reafon and Judgment may fome Sins oppofe,
And utterly refufe with them to clofe;
Yet may thy *Will*, and thy *Affections* both
To leave thofe very Sins be very loth.
If Sin be not from thy *Affections* raz'd,
Thou wilt be found an Hypocrite debas'd:

---

* Ifa. xxix. 13, &c.

For if thy *Will* in Love to Sin be found,
'Twill plainly prove thy Heart is yet unsound:
As Seamen in a Storm throw overboard
Some heavy Goods, wherewith they're over-stor'd,
Lest all their Goods, and Ship, and Lives be lost,
They'll let a Part be over Shipboard toss'd:
So in the Soul, when Storms and Tempests rise,
The Devil then may subtilly advise
The Soul to throw some of its Sins away,
To make a Calm; and thus he wins the Day;
Telling the Soul, the Danger now is o'er,
The Work is done, and he is safe on Shore:
Therefore, 'tis not enough some Sins to leave,
But ev'ry Sin thou must resolve to heave,
And cast them overboard, into the Sea
Of Christ's rich Blood, to wash them all away *:
For if thou one retain'st, tho' secretly,
'Twill sink thy Soul to all Eternity:
Nor by Constraint, thro' Fear, must this be done;
But chearfully thou must renounce each one:
For whoso shuns the Act, yet loves it still,
Forbears to act it sore against his Will:
But God abhors such a polluted Heart,
For he requires Truth in the inward Part †.

Youth.

These Sayings, *Truth*, are very hard to bear,
And they would almost drive me to Despair,
Had I not yet another Ground to shew,
Which plainly proves that my Conversion's true:

* Rev. i. 5.   † Psal. li. 6.

For, lo! in me is wrought a glorious Change,
Most Men admire it, and account it strange,
That such an one, who us'd to scoff and jeer
At God's dear Saints, whom now I love to hear,
And am accounted also one of them,
Who are the faithful Followers of the Lamb,
That I, who follow'd Vice and Vanity,
Should on a sudden thus reformed be:
And also utterly myself deny
Of all my former Sweets and Company.

TRUTH.

From outward Filthiness a Man may turn,
Yet be unchang'd; his inward Lusts may burn
Within his Heart; and longing for a Vent,
Which, when obtain'd, will send a loathsome Scent *.
An outward Change in many may be seen,
And yet their Hearts continue still unclean.
The Swine that wallow'd in the Mire just now
Is fairly wash'd, but still remains a Sow,
And quickly will, to please her foul Desire,
Return again to wallow in the Mire †.
Persons may cleanse the Outside of the Cup,
And Dogs may throw their loathsome Vomit up,
And yet their beastly Nature still retain;
For, lo! anon they lick the same again.
'Tis so with some Professors; they appear,
In outside Dress, as if true Saints they were,
And yet their Hearts are carnal and profane;
Which plainly proves they ne'er were born again.

* Psal. xxxvi. 2.   † 2 Pet. ii. 22.

This is the Cause of black Apostacy,
Because they ne'er were chang'd effectually.
Such was the boasting *Pharisee* of old,
He thought his Works were all of Sterling Gold;
Not like the *Publican*, who trembling stood,
Conscious of Guilt, before a righteous God,
He thought himself a Man of heav'nly Dress;
But all was Shew, and inward Rottenness *.
Except thy Righteousness doth his excel,
In Christ's blest Kingdom thou canst never dwell.
'Tis but a partial Change, all feign'd, not true,
Unless in thee all Things are wholly new.
King *Herod* could reform in many Things
While *Conscience* pierc'd his Heart with bitter Stings.
To hear *John Baptist* too he now seems glad;
Anon he cuts off that great Prophet's Head †.
Yea, so this seeming Saint was turn'd aside,
That Christ himself he also could deride;
And with his Men of War set him at nought,
When Accusation was against him sought ‡.
So *Simon-Magus*, when he was appriz'd
Of *Philip*'s Preaching, also was baptiz'd,
And left his Witchcraft and his forc'ring Tricks,
And with God's People he began to mix;
Yet like a painted Sepulchre was he;
An Hypocrite, e'en to the last Degree §.
Another such, O *Youth!* thou surely art,
Unless thou art renew'd in ev'ry Part;
Men in thy Life may no great Blemish spy,
While in thy Heart much Rottenness may lie.

* Luke xviii. 11. 14.   † Mark vi. 20, 29.
‡ Luke xxiii. 11.   § Acts viii. 21.

Yea, outwardly thou may'ſt ſeem very clear;
So far for thee may *Conſcience* Witneſs bear;
But towards God it ne'er will thee commend,
While yet thou doſt againſt his Laws offend;
In Thought, in Word, and Deed continually,
Still in thy Face it will with Fury fly:
For many ſecret Sins 'twill thee condemn,
Tho' none but God and *Conſcience* know of them.
Therefore, O *Youth*, 'tis Time to look about;
Of thy Converſion thou haſt Cauſe to doubt.
Take heed, leſt Satan ſhould thy Heart deceive,
And thou be found at laſt to Sin a Slave.
This is the Caſe of many of Mankind;
For ſaving Grace is very rare to find *.

YOUTH.

But I am call'd of God, and I obey
The Voice of *Truth* and *Conſcience* ev'ry Day.
And whom God calls, ev'n *Truth* cannot deny,
But they are ſuch as he will juſtify †.
Therefore 'tis clear, and ev'ry one may ſee,
That Grace alone hath made this Change in me.
My Heart is ſound, my Graces they are pure,
My Confidence built on a Rock moſt ſure,
Which none can overthrow, nor ſhake, 'twill laſt;
For my Integrity, I hold it faſt.

TRUTH.

Thy Confidence, O *Youth*, is no good Sign;
For Fears attend where ſaving Graces ſhine.

* Epheſ. ii. 5.   † Acts ii. 39.

I tell thee alfo, many called be,
But few are chofen in God's high Decree *.
Judas was call'd, and he obey'd in Part,
Yet was he but a Devil in his Heart.
 There is an outward and an inward Call,
The latter only can prevent thy Fall :
Therefore thou muft produce fome better Ground,
Ere thou canft prove that thy Foundation's found.
If thou haft not obtain'd a true new Birth,
Nothing befide will profit thee on Earth.
'Tis rare to find one truly born anew,
And harder ftill to prove the Work is true †.

YOUTH.

Well, be it fo; what Caufe have I to fear,
When, lo! my Evidences are fo clear?
For I believe, and tiuft in God thro' Faith,
Which whofo doth the inward Witnefs hath;
And may affure himfelf moft certainly,
That Heav'n is his whene'er he's call'd to die.

TRUTH.

Thou may'ft believe, as many others do,
Who yet to Hell are haft'ning downward too.
The Faith of Credence thou perhaps may'ft have,
Which cannot quicken, purify, nor fave.
Some of the *Jews* believ'd in Chrift you find,
Yet to their Lufts their Hearts were ftrong inclin'd;
And out of *Satan*'s Kingdom ne'er were freed,
Nor made Difciples of the Lord indeed.

* Matt. xx. 16.   † Matt. vii. 14.

Simon the Sorcerer thou know'ſt believ'd *,
And yet his Soul no ſaving Grace receiv'd;
But was a Child of Satan ne'ertheleſs,
And in the woful Gall of Bitterneſs †.
The *Highway Hearers*, and the *Stoney Ground*,
Receiv'd the Seed with Joy, the Goſpel-ſound;
And yet their Hearts were ſtill but Hearts of Stone;
Their Faith but temporary, quickly gone ‡.
The Devils alſo they believe 'tis true,
And they confeſs'd that Jeſus Chriſt they knew ‖:
Yea, they believe, and alſo tremble too ¶,
And that is more than ſome Profeſſors do:
And yet could they the Devils Faith obtain,
'Twould ſerve no Turn, but to augment their Pain.
If on a Death-bed *Conſcience* ſhould awake,
With what amazing Horror would they quake!
And roar like Devils, when with Grief they 'ſpy
The dreadful Wrath, and glorious Majeſty,
Of that great **God**, whom they, for all their Light,
Have long rebell'd againſt with Main and Might.

Their Faith but ſerves to aggravate their Grief,
But never will afford the leaſt Relief.
'Tis eaſy to believe that Chriſt hath dy'd,
But, ah, how hard to get his blood apply'd!
Men may as eaſy raiſe the Dead again,
As of themſelves true ſaving Faith obtain §:
For all their Wit, their Learning and their Skill;
Nothing obſtructs it more than Man's own Will;
'Till God's almighty Pow'r makes that to bend,
'Twill not an Ear to Chriſt the Saviour lend:

* Acts viii. 13.   † Acts viii. 23.   ‡ Matt. xiii. 4, 5, 6.
‖ Mark v. 7.   ¶ James ii. 19.   § Eph. ii. 5——8.

No Pow'r but that which rais'd him from the Dead,
Works Faith in Saints, and quickens with their Head.
A Faith of Credence, verbally believ'd,
Is easy found and readily receiv'd:
But precious Faith, the Faith of God's Elect *,
Wherewith Christ's Spouse is inwardly bedeck'd;
With other Graces, this will ne'er be found,
But in the honest Heart by Grace made sound.
This blessed Seed, sow'd in a Garden pure;
Yields timely Fruit, and endless shall endure.

  Now when this Faith in any one is wrought,
That Soul is truly to Christ Jesus brought:
Then is he only its beloved one,
Whom it receives, and wholly rests upon.
Now if the Lord this Gift hath given thee,
Sin thou abhor'st, and all Iniquity:
Nor doth one Lust predominate and reign,
If thou by Faith art truly born again.
Christ is thy Prophet, Priest, and only King,
And thou to him submit'st in ev'ry Thing.
He doth in thee his Sceptre freely sway,
And thou art govern'd by him Night and Day †.
Sin can't prevail, such is thy happy Case,
If thou hast got this rare victorious Grace.
It purges fair, and purifies the Heart,
Wholly renewing it in ev'ry Part,
Man by its Fruits true Faith can only know ‡;
It works by Love, its Fruits for ever grow.

  Now, *Youth*, what Faith is thine? what think'st of it?
Dost thou not fear 'twill prove a Counterfeit?

* Tit. i. 1.   † Isa. xxxiii. 22.   ‡ Jam. ii. 20, 21, 22.

Examine well thy State, and take good Heed,
To know if thou art yet in Christ indeed:
For as the Body, when the Spirit's gone,
Is dead; so is the Faith of ev'ry one,
When new Obedience, don't his Faith attend *;
And all his Confidence with Shame will end.

YOUTH.

But I'm obedient too; and free to join
In Fellowship with Saints; such Faith *is* mine,
That I obey as willing as believe:
Therefore the Devil can't my Soul deceive;
Yea, I have clos'd with Christ; not only so,
I'm built on him; none can my Faith o'erthrow.
The many Prayers I make both Day and Night,
Likewise confirms that my Conversion's right.

TRUTH.

Alas, poor *Youth!* Men may do more than this,
And after all of true Conversion miss.
God's Ordinances many seem t' obey,
And out-side Members of his Church are they:
Of outward Privileges they may Share,
As much as those who real Converts are:
They may discourse, and seem to be devout;
So that no Man on Earth can find them out:
They with the Flock may walk, lie down and feed,
Year after Year, from outward Censures freed;
'Till unsuspected they're compell'd to stand
Amongst the Goats at last on Christ's left Hand.

* Jam. ii. 26.

Examples of Self-Deception.

The foolish Virgins with the wise repose,
And at the Midnight-Cry they all arose
To meet the Bride-Groom; but before he came
They wanted Oil; they found it to their Shame:
The Wise had Oil; but none to give or lend;
Nor fell the Foolish: Now they apprehend
All their Religion is a bare out-side,
That never would the Test of Truth abide ‡.

So many Preachers and Disputers too,
Christ will at last no real Favour shew;
Though mighty Works they in his Name have done,
He'll then pronounce, " Ye faithless ones, begone,
" I know you not; therefore depart from me,
" All ye vile Workers of Iniquity †."
Thou say'st, thou often seek'st the Lord by Pray'r;
That thou may'st do, and yet have Cause to fear;
For this thou may'st, though unregenerate,
As *Esau* fought with Tears when 'twas too late:
Or *Seamen* like, when hideous Storms arise;
While *Death* and *Conscience* fill them with Surprize.
Many, when under sore Afflictions, howl,
And grievously their wretched States condole;
Fair Promises, and Resolutions make
That they their sinful Courses will forsake:
But when the Storm of their Affliction's o'er,
They grow as hard, nay harder than before.

Some pray by Form; and others pray by Art;
And some to ease, or heal a broken Heart:
Their Hearts are wounded, then they speedily
A Pray'r Balsam unto the Wound apply.

‡ Matt. xxv. 1——13. † Matt. vii. 22, 23.

They

They sin all Day, and then they pray at Night,
They sin again, but Pray'r soon sets 'em right.
They think 'tis well if many Tears they strain,
For Tears and Prayers cures all their sharpest Pain.
And thus poor *Conscience* they at once beguile
To Silence, tho' they're Sinners all the while:
But, ah! how they their precious Souls deceive;
For greater Condemnation they must have.
Their Pray'rs and Tears will never wash away
Their sinful Stains, could they both Night and Day
Do nothing else; yet if they rest thereon,
'Twill prove a broken Reed to lean upon.

A real Saint can here no Ease obtain;
Nought but the Blood of Christ will heal his Pain:
Nothing his parching Thirst will satisfy,
But real Grace, his Lusts to mortify.
Not so the Natural-Man, whose partial Cry
Is still for Pardon, whilst he secretly
Still hugs his Sins within his Heart most dear,
Therefore the Lord his Pray'rs will never hear:
For all their splendid Duties are abhorr'd,
Who strive to hide their Secrets from the Lord †.

Some out of Custom many Prayers make,
And others only for vain-glory's Sake,
Like *Pharisees* they love to pray aloud,
And to be seen and heard of Men they're proud:
But in the Closet they are seldom found;
Except it be when Standers-by abound ‡.

And some to God will frequently draw near,
Not out of Love, nor out of filial Fear;

† Luke xii. 2. Isa. xxix. 14. ‡ Matt. vi. 5.

Yet

Yet with their Lips and Tongues much Kindness show,
While their false Hearts are set on Things below:
But this won't do, for God the Heart requires,
Which if refus'd, he nothing else desires §:
'Tis his own Right, he purchas'd it most dear,
Though Satan keeps his grand Possession there.
God at the Door, or in the Porch may stand;
While Satan can the chiefest Rooms command:
They'll ope' to him, and keep JEHOVAH out;
And yet in Pray'r they will appear devout.

Some often pray and keep a constant Round,
Tho' Soul and Body both asleep be found:
But whoso prays, and prays not fervently
In *Faith*, in *Hope*, and in true *Charity*;
Their Prayers are to God Abomination,
For he abhors their specious Supplication *.
'Tis not enough to keep a constant Round
Of sev'ral Duties, with an empty Sound:
For Men may read, pray, hear and meditate,
And yet continue in a graceless State:
Many great Truths they may in Words profess,
Who never felt the Power of Godliness.
The Letter of the Law they may retain,
Yet in the Gall of Bitterness remain.
The specious *Youth* that once to Jesus came,
Had kept the Law quite free from outward Blam;
And yet fell short; as thou may'st plainly see ‡,
For not one Dram of Saving-Grace had he.

Now what say'st thou, O *Youth?* pray search and see,
Lest thou by Satan still deceiv'd should'st be.

§ 1 Chron. xxviii. 9.   * Isa. i. 15.   ‡ Mark x. 17.

Haft thou no *Delilah* thou hug'ft within?
No ftrong Affection to fome bofom Sin?
If ftill thou doft fome fecret Sin retain,
This plainly proves thou art not born again *.
If *Confcience* and Reftraining-Grace with Fear,
Have only ftopt thee in thy mad Career;
Like furious Dogs confin'd by hamp'ring Chains,
Whofe vicious Nature ftill the fame remains:
So, if thy finful Nature be not chang'd,
Thou art, and muft be ftill, from God eftrang'd,
 In thy own Righteoufnefs doft thou not truft?
Speak and declare, or *Confcience* furely muft.
Doft thou not think that God's oblig'd to thee,
Since thou reformed haft to this Degree?
Are not thy Duties fet up in Chrift's Place?
Examine well if this be not the Cafe.
Did ever Sin in its own hue appear;
Filling thy Soul with deep Remorfe and Fear;
So that the flighteft Touch of that foul Stain,
Would pierce thy Soul with Horror, Shame and Pain?
And that becaufe 'tis loathfome in God's Sight,
Therefore thou hat'ft it with thy Mind and Might?
But if it be the Fear of Punifhment,
Which makes thee now thy former Sins refent;
'Tis to be fear'd thou haft fome bafe Defign,
Which makes thee with God's holy People join.
Is not thy Aim to get a Name thereby?
Or teafing *Confcience* thus to pacify?
Or elfe to fcreen thee from Reproach and Shame,
Which many Sins bring on a Perfon's Name?

   * Ifa. lviii. 2.

Or is not all this Shyness, and Remorse
Against thy Sins, only to save thy Purse?
For wild luxurious Living in this Age,
Consumes the Stock, and Mis'ries dire presage.
   Is this thy Case, O *Youth*? I pray be free;
Hide not the Secrets of thy Heart from me.
Call now to Mind what thou hast heard of late,
And thereby judge of this thy present State.

YOUTH.

I can't see yet but my Condition's good,
I have such Faith and Hope in Jesus' Blood.
Though many Imperfections in me be,
Yet God is gracious and will pardon me:
For many Failings in the Best are found,
Therefore I hope my State is safe and found.

TRUTH.

   Thy Trust, O *Youth*, is in the Spider's Web!
Thy Tide of Hope will have a dreadful Ebb*,
If thou prove guilty of those Things which I
Did in thine Ear so lately specify,
Thy Spots will not be like the Spots of those
Which God for Children to himself hath chose.
But since thou art so backward to be try'd,
It seems thou aim'st some secret Crimes to hide;
Therefore to *Conscience* I'll again appeal,
To hear what he against thee can reveal:
For he's enlighten'd now; he can declare
As much as we at present need to hear.
He'll speak the Truth, and righteous Judgment give,
Nor hide if thou in secret Sin dost live.

      * Job viii. 14.

Therefore attend unto his faithful Voice;
If he acquit thee, then thou mayſt rejoice:
But if againſt thee he ſhould Witneſs bear,
Depend upon it thou haſt Cauſe to fear.
And if thou wilt not hear what he ſhall ſay,
He'll make thee tremble at the Judgment-Day.

  Now, *Conſcience*, in the Name of our great King,
I call thee forth thy Evidence to bring
Againſt this Man; accuſe or, ſet him free
According to the Light thou haſt from me.
Stand up for Chriſt thy only ſov'reign Lord,
And Judgment give according to his Word.
Be not deceiv'd by Luſt: all Bribes forſake;
And judge by Law: Chriſt's Honour lies at Stake.
Speak loud, ſpeak home, if thou haſt not forgot,
Is he converted yet? or is he not?
What doſt thou ſay? thy Teſtimony give;
Are his Luſts dead? or do there any live?
Is he new-born, and chang'd in ev'ry Part?
Or but in outward Shew, and not in Heart?

CONSCIENCE.

  Hold! ſay no more; I am at thy Command;
And I'll declare how Things at preſent ſtand.
He hath, O *Truth*, almoſt deceived me,
By late Appearances of Sanctity:
But having now receiv'd of thee more Light,
I muſt declare he's but an Hypocrite.
He is not yet renew'd, nor born again,
As I ſhall ſoon with Verity explain.
For firſt of all, his Faculty call'd *Will*,
Is moſt perverſe, and very ſtubborn ſtill.

Tho' I excite to Duties ev'ry Hour,
Will, still opposes me with all its Pow'r.
He never prays in secret Day nor Night,
Except I force him to it with a Fright.
The old Man is not slain, I plainly see;
But has much Favour shown him secretly:
And tho' to Holes I force him oft to run,
Yet in the Heart he still maintains his Throne.
His strong *Affections* still are set on Sin,
And so indeed they ever yet have been.
His Pangs for Sin spring all from slavish Fear,
Not for the Evil that is rooted there.

When he's abroad amongst religious Men;
Precise, and zealous he is always then:
But when among th' Ungodly he appears,
He suits his Language to their carnal Ears.

Some Sins are left by him which men count gross,
Others he keeps, and hugs them very close.
One Lust bears Rule, and strong predominates,
And still on it he dotes, and ruminates.
'Tis Shame, or slavish Fear, makes him restrain;
Or he would freely act the same again.
If he from outward Blots can keep his Name;
That Saints, nor Sinners, can him justly blame;
He's satisfy'd, and very well content;
Tho' to his Peace I never gave consent.

Peace oft he speaks to his deluded Soul;
Nor will he bear of me the least controul.
Sometimes I catch him in a horrid Lie,
And sharp reprove him for Hypocrisy:
To stop my Mouth, he vows he will amend
What e'er's amiss, and me no more offend.

Yea, *Truth*, of him I could much more relate,
And shew how thou haft hit his prefent State ;
But lo, he ftops my Mouth, nor lets me fpeak ;
And blinds mine eyes, left I his Peace fhould break :
For if I fhew'd all his Iniquity,
He would fuftain amazing lofs thereby.

TRUTH.

Confcience, forbear, thou need'ft no more enlarge ;
Since all thefe Things thou doft againft him charge
He is undone : Alas! his precious Soul
Is under Wrath ; who can enough condole
His fad Eftate ! for all his outward Drefs
Still is he in the Gall of Bitternefs.
Is this the Man that feem'd a Saint precife ;
And did appear God's Statutes much to prize ?
A Saint in Shew, a Devil in his Heart,
And muft with fuch for ever have his Part ;
If he continue in this direful State,
Then muft he die a wretched Reprobate!
The Day is coming ; yea, 'tis very near,
When Hypocrites fhall be furpriz'd with Fear,
And their Abode they muft for ever take
Amidft the Flames of Hell's prodigious Lake *.
But fince thou art not fear'd ; nor I yet gone,
Confcience, awake, and I'll with thee fet on,
And we'll purfue him ftill ; for who can tell
But God may yet his num'rous Sins expel ?
Should God beftow one Dram of faving Grace,
'Twould him reftore ; tho' 'tis a doubtful Cafe,

* Ifa. xxviii. 14.

Whether or not he will his Grace afford,
To such an Hypocrite; a Wretch abhor'd:
For such whom Satan doth this Way deceive,
'Tis rare to bring them truly to believe.
  He never has aright convicted been
Of the destructive nature of his Sin.
His lost Estate, he never truly saw,
Nor what it was to break God's holy Law*.
How he's undone thereby he never knew;
Nor what was to his sinful Nature due ‡.
And as for Sin he ne'er did truely bleed,
So he of Christ hath never seen his Need §:
The great Necessity of his rich Blood
To purge his Stains, he never understood:
But on false Bottoms he hath built his Tow'r,
And is deceived to this very Hour.
Conscience, I now conjure thee, do not spare;
But his great Danger fully now declare:
That he is all unclean from Top to Toe †;
Make him to understand and fully know.
The Plague is in his Head, and no Place free,
But in his Heart it rages dreadfully.
Lance him unto the Quick, and make him feel
Thy probing Instruments, and wond'rous skill.

CONSCIENCE.

Come, O vain *Youth*, attend again on me;
I can no longer thus deceived be.

   * Gal. iii. 10.   ‡ Rom. viii. 7.
   § Matt. ix. 12.   † Isa. i. 6.

A fresh Commission from the Word of Truth
I have receiv'd, and must declare, O *Youth!*
And this new Message, which I bring to thee,
'Twill surely make thee tremble, faint, or flee:
For all thy high flown Hopes, and goodly Dress;
Still thou art in the Gall of Bitterness.
Thou think'st on *Conscience* to commit a Rape;
And yet God's righteous Vengeance to escape.
And dar'st thou thus, under a new Disguise,
Try to deceive me with thy Subtilties:
Ah! thou art still the same, howe'er of late,
Thou'st chang'd thy Coat, the Eyes of Men to cheat.
Ungodly Wretch! dost thou not dread to hear
My Voice? who am against thee to declare
A second War; and I must let thee know
That God is still thy most enraged Foe.
His Sword his drawn, his Bow is also bent,
To cut thee off, except thou dost repent;
For nothing is more odious in his Eye
Than fair Outsides, and Heart Hypocrisy.

YOUTH.

Conscience, be still, though I a Sinner be,
There's none knows of it now but only thee.

CONSCIENCE.

Deluded Soul! does none thy Guilt descry,
Save me alone? Where's then thy Maker's Eye!
Dost think from him, behind a sable Cloud
Thy secret Crimes, and inward Thoughts to shroud?
Behold the Beams of his all-piercing Eye
Dart through the darkest Clouds that veil the Sky.

He tries the Reins; he searches ev'ry Part;
Displays the deep Recesses of the Heart.
And can'st thou be so vain to think that none
Beholds thy secret Sins but me alone!
And know'st thou not that I'm in Pow'r to use
Authority, t' acquit thee or accuse * ?
I must impartially the Truth declare,
When thou art summon'd to thy M ker's Bar.
Should I be still, 'twould be a dreadful Day;
Unless thy sins were wholly purg'd away.
And whilst I speak, and thou refrain'st to hear
Nothing but Terror will accost thine Ear.
I'll never side with thee, nor take thy Part,
While secret Guilt is harbour'd in thy Heart.
Nor would I mind thy Flatt'ry or thy Frown,
Wast thou a Prince of most sublime Renown,
That ever did on Earth the Scepter sway;
Before thy Face, thy secret Faults I'd lay.
At smallest Sins I never will connive;
Therefore with me it is in vain to strive:
For lo, I am a Monitor severe,
And whoso won't my Admonitions hear,
To them I am a constant Enemy,
From whom they never can at Distance fly.
Thy Thoughts, thy Words, thy Deeds, whate'er they be;
However secret they're well known to me.
Thy lustful Acts conceal'd in sable Night,
Of which thou art asham'd should come to Light,
I plainly see, nor will I more conceal
One secret Sin, but will them all reveal.

* Rom. ii. 15.

For while thou doft indulge Iniquity,
I fhall be ftill thy bitter Enemy.
When Sicknefs comes; and Death ftares in thy Face,
Then will I fill thy Soul with deep Difgrace.
The Bill of thy Indictment will be large,
For then I'll bring in fuch a dreadful Charge,
As fhall produce in thee a woful Look,
And wound thy Heart as if 'twere Thunder-ftruck.
Thy Pleafures then I'll into Sadnefs turn,
And make thee rue the Day that thou waft born.
Nay, to thy fatal Coft thou then fhalt know
What 'tis to have thy *Confcience* be thy Foe.

Again give Ear; for I have more to fay,
When Death has done; lo there's another Day;
Another Day of Terror is to come,
Ah! difmal Scene! the dreadful Day of Doom!
And there will I a Witnefs fwift appear,
To fill thy Soul with Horror, Grief, and Fear.
And when among the Goats at Chrift's Left-hand;
There I a Terror fhall againft thee ftand:
Accufing thee before the Judgment-Seat;
Where none fhall pity thy forlorn Eftate.
Then fhall I fpeak more clear than now I can;
Becaufe I'm clouded by the Fall of Man;
And am by Satan oftentimes beguil'd:
And through blind Ignorance with Sin defil'd.
Then weak in Judgment I remain awhile,
Till *Truth* breaks in, and purges me from Guile:
Then Satan over me no Pow'r can have,
Whereby he may the Hearts of Men deceive.
But, *Youth*, in that great Day of deep Diftrefs,
I'll make thy Lips, with Grief and Shame confefs,

Thy

The Hypocrite's Alarm.

Thy secret Crimes, and close Hypocrisy,
Before thy Judge's all tremendous Eye!
Yea, there thy Secrets all, shall open'd be,
And nothing hid from the great Judge and me.
E'en all thy Crimes that were in Darkness done
Shall be disclos'd before the blazing Sun.
And I shall so confound thee in that Day
That for thyself one Word thou can'st not say.
And then the dreadful Sentence thou must hear,
More shocking than a thousand Deaths to bear.
" Go, thou accursed, *saith the Judge*, retire,
" And take thy Dwelling in eternal Fire;
" Where Hypocrites, and Unbeliever's lie,
" With Devil's howling to Eternity."
And when thou thus by him condemned art
I'll go with thee, and hang upon thy Heart,
And like a deathless Worm, or Viper bite,
And gnaw thy Soul, thou faithless Hypocrite.
My inward Stings thou must for ever feel,
Far worse than Whips of everlasting Steel.
Which will increase, and aggravate thy woe,
In such a Sort as Words can never show.

Then shalt thou call to mind how thou'st abus'd
Thy *Conscience*; and his kind Advice refus'd.
And how thou labour'st to put out my Light,
When in God's Ways I strove to lead thee right.
Thy base Delays, and Put-offs then lament;
And happy Seasons foolishly misspent.
And that the Love, which thou to Lust did'st bear,
Should plunge thy Soul in such a dreadful Snare.
To think thou wast so near the happy Gate,
Will grievously thy Troubles aggravate.

To bid so fair for Heaven, and yet to miss,
What can a greater Trouble be than this!
Nothing can vex the worldly Merchant more
Than see his Ship wreck'd almost at the Shore.
 I'll tell thee also how thou wilfully
Brought'st on thyself this endless Misery:
And how I did so frequently declare
What for those Sins thou must for ever bear,
And what thy fav'rite Lusts would bring thee to
If thou would'st not consent to let them go.
Ah! thou wilt see thyself at last undone,
And all thy Hopes for ever fled and gone.
How will thy Mind be then with Terror tost
To think what golden Seasons thou hast lost!
And how thou might'st, had'st thou not shun'd his Grace,
Beheld, with Saints, God's reconciled Face;
And enter'd his bless'd Courts, where Angels sing
Celestial Songs to him their God and King;
And might'st have join'd the glorious Concert there,
Whose Hands triumphant Palms for ever bear;
And on whose Heads eternal Crowns shall be,
Reigning with Christ through all Eternity.
Nay, what's all this! Heaven's Glories far excel
What Man can think, much more what Tongue can [tell:
For Truth declares, *Man's Heart can ne'er conceive*
The Joys of those who do on Christ believe*.
 O then what Fools are those who slight this Prize,
For short liv'd Lusts, and fair delusive lies!
But if what's said of Heav'n won't thee invite,
See if Hell's Torments will not thee affright;

* 1 Cor. ii. 9.

          And

And make thee yield to Truth without Delay
Before thou art by Vengeance snatch'd away.
For as Man's Heart can't think nor Tongue express
The great Reward which Saints in Heaven possess,
So neither can they ever fully know
The vast extent of Hell's eternal woe.
If Man could number all the Stars of Heav'n,
Or count the Dust, and Leaves by Tempests driv'n;
Or tell the Drops of Water in the Seas;
Or Sands upon the Shore; with equal Ease
Might he declare the Greatness of that Pain
Which damned Souls for ever must sustain.
But as these Things could never yet be done
By any Man on Earth; e'en so can none
Express the Weight of God's Almighty Wrath
Which Souls lie under in eternal Death.

Lo, there is Darkness, not one Beam of Light!
And what's more dreadful than eternal Night?
Yea, there is Death; and yet the soul ne'er dies!
And nought is heard but hid'ous Shrieks and Cries.
Their Pains are great, yet can it ne'er be dream'd
That from their Mis'ries they shall be redeem'd.
Their Cries procure no Help, no tender Eye
Laments the Greatness of their Misery.
There's all Despair, and not one Beam of Hope;
There's burning Throats, but not one cooling Drop.
They're given up, nor can they e'er repent,
Therefore their Miseries God cannot prevent.

Now all Despisers of his rich Free-grace,
Must have their Portion in that dreadful Place.
But all that Men can paint can ne'er declare
The woful Anguish of the Damned there.

For

For if these Pains could be defin'd by Men,
They could not be unmeasurable then.
Infinite Wrath is to be satisfy'd,
And God's strict Justice must be magnify'd.
Did'st thou but hear the Noise, the hid'ous Cry
Of damned Souls that in these Torments lie:
How would it fear thee to behold that Lake,
And cause each Limb to tremble, fear and quake!
O think on this, before the Time shall come,
That God shall pass on thee the final Doom.

TRUTH.

Youth, what say'st now? ah! canst thou rest in Pe
Until these inward Pangs of *Conscience* cease *?
How canst thou think or dream thy State is good
While *Conscience* swells and raises such a Flood?
He raises Storms and Tempests in thy Breast;
Because of Sin he will not let thee rest.

Come search thy Heart; *Conscience* is not misled;
The very Truth before thee he hath spread.
What wilt thou do at the great Judgment-Day,
If thou should'st still his Counsel disobey?
Make Peace with him; for louder are his Cries
Than if ten thousand Witnesses should rise
Against thy Soul: Ah! what a dreadful Thing
Should he against thee his last Verdict bring.

YOUTH.

Shew Pity, *Truth*, alas! my Soul will melt;
Such Pangs as these my Heart-strings never felt.

* Isa. lvii. 20, 21.

To Doubting Caſtle I at laſt am brought;
I fear Converſion ne'er in me was wrought.
My Heart condemns me: *Conſcience* wounds me ſore;
O *Truth*, remove my Burden I implore!

TRUTH.

Before thou haſt a Plaiſter for thy Wound,
Thy Ulcers muſt be ſearch'd, and firſt made Sound,
If ſlightly heal'd, to give thee preſent Eaſe,
The Cure will prove yet worſe than the Diſeaſe*.
Doſt know what Time thou didſt this Wound receive?
'Tis worſe, I fear, than yet thou canſt believe.
'Tis deep, it ſtinks, it putrifies and grows,
And to eternal Wrath will thee expoſe.
The Law's ſharp Arrow; its tremendous Dart
Has forc'd its Entrance to thy carnal Heart.
Thy State is bad, thou'ſt got thy mortal Wound;
No Part within thee, nor without is found †.
Could'ſt thou now live, and never more tranſgreſs,
Yet would the Law condemn thee ne'ertheleſs:
For could'ſt thou hence from actual Sins keep clear,
This ne'er would pay thy former long Arrear.
Thy former Crimes, which are of Crimſon Dye,
Would ſtill to Heav'n aloud for Vengeance cry.
Juſtice will never pardon nor reprieve
One Soul, till Satisfaction it receive. ‡.

Againſt thy Soul the dreadful Doom is paſt,
Nor may thy Reſpite for a Moment laſt.
There's nothing now 'twixt thee and endleſs Death,
But ſome few Moments of uncertain Breath ‖.

* Jer. vi. 14. † Iſa. i. 6. ‡ Matt. v. 26. ‖ *Pſ.* xc. 5, 6, 7.

Sin is so vile, and Justice so severe,
That Christ himself it would in no wise spare,
When in the guilty Sinner's Place he stood,
Lo, it requir'd its full Demand in Blood *:
And since in Christ thou hast obtain'd no Part,
A wretched, poor, condemned Soul thou art.

YOUTH.

O cursed Sin! now I begin to see
How thou hast ruin'd, and deluded me:
Truth has made known how thou hast led me wrong,
Altho' Convictions in me have been strong.
O horrid Lusts, and base deceitful Devil!
Is this the fruit of all your pleasing Evil?
And thou false World; ah! what art thou to me?
Alas! alas! I'm quite undone by thee.
O whither shall I flee! what path untrod
Shall I find out to shun the wrath of God!
Will none for me some secret Cave provide
Where from his flaming Vengeance I might hide?

TRUTH.

Vain Thought, alas! where can'st thou find a Place
To hide thee from thy Maker's angry Face?
Could'st thou arise on Morning Wings, and fly
To the remotest Verge beneath the Sky;
How vain the Thought, to 'scape his mighty Hand,
Without whose Aid thou canst not move or stand!
Or should'st thou think beneath the sable Night,
To screen thee safe from his all-piercing Sight:

* Matt. xxvii. 39, 42, 44.

Fruitless

Fruitless Attempt! for, lo, he sees as soon.
Through midnight Shades as in the Blaze of Noon.
Or should'st thou dare presume to stop thy Breath,
And shun his Eye amongst the Shades of Death:
Worse Madness still! for to his Majesty,
Death, Grave, and Hell without a cov'ring lie.
Caves, Rocks, nor Seas can hide thee from his Ire,
For at his Presence those shall all expire *.
Then think no more thou canst a Place descry
To shroud thee from his bright omniscient Eye.

YOUTH.

O *Truth!* what shall I do? how shall I stand,
To bear the Stroke of God's vindictive Hand?
A Man's own Strength his Frailties may outwear,
But, O! a wounded Spirit who can bear †?
But is there *Truth*, no *Balm*, to heal my Wound,
In *Gilead*? is there no *Physician* found ‡?
Will Pray'rs and Tears to me no Help afford?
Nor watching, fasting, hearing of the Word?
If all these Duties will not ease my Grief,
Where shall I go to seek and find Relief?
O whether shall I flee! or where explore,
A Remedy for Sin, my Gangrene-sore?
O what's the Nature of Iniquity,
That nought will cleanse me of this **Leprosy**?
Rivers of Oil, much Gold and worldly **Wealth**,
I see avail not to restore my Health.
  Ah! I am lost! I see 'tis plainly so!
Undone! undone! O *Truth*, where shall I go?

* Psal. cxxxix. 1—12. † Prov. xviii. 14. Jer. viii. 22.

Hast thou no Word of Comfort yet for me?
Or must I perish to Eternity?

TRUTH.

And dost thou feel at last the cutting Smart
Of my sharp Arrows piercing thy hard Heart?
Does Sin as Sin upon thy Spirits lie,
The Weight of which makes thee lament and cry?
Dost know the Danger of thy dire Disease?
And that there's none on Earth that can appease
The Wrath of God? Ah! dost thou see thy Loss?
And thine own Righteousness but Dung and Dross †?

YOUTH.

I know not what to say, I'm still in Doubt,
Lest yet some secret Sin I've not found out.
My Heart is deep and most deceitful too,
Alas! alas! I know not what to do.
I grieve for Sin, and yet I am in Dread,
That Sin in me is not yet wholly dead.
Yet this O *Truth*, I hope is wrought in me,
Sin I abhor, as 'tis Iniquity:
Nor would I Christ offend or grieve again,
Were there no Hell to fear, or future Pain.
Ah! how I fear lest I again should sin,
Against the Lord who hath so gracious been,
To spare my Life; nor cut me off so soon,
For all the heinous Evils I have done.
But ah! I see that I in Sin am dead,
And my Iniquities gone o'er my Head.

† Isa. lxiv. 6. Phil. iii. 8.

He is jealous of himself.

O could I now but of a Saviour hear!
For, lo, my Load is more than I can bear,
Now my own Righteousness I prize no more
Than stinking Filth upon a common Shore.
All I have done has but enhanc'd my Woe:
Alas! I'm helpless, whether shall I go?

TRUTH.

And is it so, O *Youth*, in every Deed,
That now thy sin-sick Soul begins to bleed?
Come then, chear up, glad News to thee I bring;
Here's a free Pardon from thy heavenly King.
Behold, his Anger's turn'd away from thee;
For Christ hath paid thy Ransom on the Tree*.
Therefore arise, poor Soul, arise and come,
For I am sent t' invite thee welcome Home.
Come, for the Spirit will Christ's Blood apply,
And that will cure each hurtful Malady†.

YOUTH.

O *Truth*, could I thy cheering Words believe,
How sweetly would it my poor Soul relieve!
But, ah! on me there's such a Burden lies,
It bows me down; I have no Pow'r to rise.
Could *Laz'rus* rouse himself, or move, or try
Death's Fetters strong from his frail Limbs t' unty?
Could he awake? What Pow'r had he to strive,
When dead and stinking? Could he then revive?
No! though but four Days dead: Then how shall I,
Who have lain dead in my Iniquity,

* Job xxxiii. 24.   † 1 John i. 7.

Ever

Ever since *Adam*'s Fall (which now appears
To be above five Thousand long, long Years)
Rise from the Death of Sin? Ah! God must take
The Work into his Hand, who first did make,
This stony Heart of mine, must form anew,
Ere any Good will to my Soul accrue.
'Tis he alone must Will and Pow'r command,
And Life infuse, ere I can walk or stand.

TRUTH.

'Tis true, frail *Youth*; yet lend an Ear to me,
And wholsome Counsel I'll impart to thee;
And thou shalt find, as sure as God is Love,
Thy Fears and Fetters quickly he'll remove;
And raise thee up from this deep miry Pit,
And on a stable Rock confirm thy Feet*.

Now my Advice, which first I recommend,
Is, Take heed *Conscience* thou no more offend.
Grieve him no more, but take abundant Care
To prove thyself in ev'ry Thing sincere:
For whoso deals deceitfully with God,
Must surely fall beneath his angry Rod.
But, lo, their happy Lot, who fear the Lord,
In ev'ry Land, and tremble at his Word,
Is this, to them he shews his smiling Face,
But fills *Dissemblers* with their own Disgrace †.
And whoso follows on to know the Lord,
His saving Health he will in Time afford.

Next I advise thee, in the second Place,
With Diligence attend the Means of Grace.

* Psal. xl. 2. † Isa. lxvi. 2, 5.

And good Advice to Youth's *troubled Soul.*

Never God's blessed Word when preach'd despise,
But all such happy Seasons richly prize:
For in his House, the Lord is often found,
And makes the heavy Heart with Joy abound*.
  My third Advice is this, continually
Be much in Pray'r unto the Lord most high.
Pour out thy Soul before him Night and Day ‡;
He'll surely answer though he long delay:
Yea, tho' thou may'st with sharp Repulses meet,
Still prostrate lie at great *Immanuel*'s Feet:
His Bowels of Compassion soon will move,
Nor can he cease to manifest his Love
To thy poor Soul; nor will he let thee lie,
Without the Pity of his tender Eye.
Yea, he the good *Physician* will be found,
Who will apply a Plaister to thy Wound,
Which cannot fail to make thee safe and sound.
Altho' thy Wounds are such, when understood,
Nought will avail thee but his precious Blood:
Yet know tho' *Priest* and *Levite* pass thee by,
This good *Samaritan*, with gracious Eye,
Will look on thee, and fill those Wounds of thine,
With richer Cordials far than *Oil* and *Wine* §.
  Lastly, for *Grace* my Sister earnestly
Lift up thy Voice: God will not thee deny,
But send her down to be thy constant Friend,
And kind Assistant to thy Journey's End ∥.
Yea, she'll advance thee to sublime Renown,
And on thy Temples set the royal Crown.

    * Rom. x. 17.   ‡ Thes. v. 17.
    § Luke x. 31,——35. ∥ Prov. ii. 6.

But here beware lest thou be put to Shame,
For there are two who both assume the Name:
The one a Counterfeit, unchaste, impure *;
The other true, unchangeable and sure †.
The one will dwell where Sin predominates;
The other ev'ry Sin abominates.
She makes a thorough Change where e'er she dwells,
And from the Heart each sinful Lust expels.
Such is th' Effect of real *Saving-Grace*,
Wherever she takes up her dwelling Place.
Thy stubborn *Will* she'll make submit by Love,
And thy *Affections* set on Things above:
New mould thy Heart, and each unruly Thought,
Shall by her Skill be to Subjection brought.
Thy *Oldman-Nature* wholly she'll cashier,
And none of all his specious Trump'ry spare.
She'll put the Works of Darkness all to Flight,
Yea, all that's opposite to Truth and Light.
She'll make the Devil's Garrison give Way,
And what is left destroy, burn down, or slay.
She'll have no Pity on the *Oldman*'s Age,
But pay him off for all his Wrath and Rage,
His cruel Malice, Pride, and ev'ry Sin,
Of which he hath the cruel Author been,
In his own Coin, and send him strait away,
Nor give him Quarters 'till another Day.

She'll also change thy avaricious Heart,
And make thee freely of thy Wealth impart,
To feed the Hungry, and to cloath the Bare,
Whereof before thou wast so loth to spare ‡.

* Luke xii. 1.   † John i. 17-   ‡ Luke xix. 8.

'Tis she brings down the haughty furious Mind,
And makes it humble, patient, meek, resign'd.
'Tis she that tames th' unruly headstrong Youth,
And makes them hearken to the Word of Truth:
Quenches their mad ungovern'd lustful Fires,
And makes 'em hate their former lew'd Desires.
She mollifies the Heart, gives *Conscience* peace,
And makes the loud tempestuous Billows cease *.
'Tis she must put Christ's spotless Robes on thee,
And from the Yoke of Bondage set thee free,
'Tis she must thee adorn and beautify,
And make thee lovely in the Bridegroom's Eye ‡.
'Tis she that can thy Soul with Love enflame,
To Christ alone, and other Loves disclaim.
'Tis She must tie the blessed Marriage Knot,
'Twixt Christ and thee, which ne'er shall be forgot:
Nor can it e'er be broken or unty'd
When truly knit, both Parties satisfy'd:
For she makes Christ and true Believers one;
Partakers of one Spirit, Flesh and Bone §.

   Thus Christ's Disciple thou shalt be indeed,
Grace will supply thy Wants in Time of Need.
But this, O *Youth*, thou must implore by Pray'r ╪,
And that believing God will lend an Ear;
For since for thee the Prince of Glory dy'd,
Of nothing needful shalt thou be deny'd ‖.
O! cease not then this Favour to implore,
But beg of God thy heav'nly Father more
Of his rich *Grace*, to ease thy Soul of Pain,
And fairly prove that thou art born again.

  * 2 Cor. xii. 9.   ‡ Psal. xlv. 13, 14, 15.   † Eph. ii. 8.
  § Eph. v. 30.   ╪ Ezek. xxxvi. 37.   ‖ Rom. viii. 32.

Be earnest then, and strive to hold him fast,
And thou like *Jacob* shalt prevail at last *.
Tho' at the first he seem to stop his Ear,
Yet Faith and Fervency will make him hear ‡ :
For this to thee is sure a Time of Love,
And thy deep Wounds will his kind Bowels move
To ease thy Pain; he'll cast a tender Eye,
Whilst thou polluted in thy Blood dost lie ;
And what is needful freely he will give :
Tho' dead he'll breath in Life, and bid thee live §.
Yea, manifest his precious Love to thee
And clothe thy Soul with his Salvation free.
Come make a Trial then ; renounce Despair:
Look up to Heav'n, dear Soul, thy Help is there.

YOUTH.

Thanks for thy Counsel, *Truth* ; I'll now take hee
T'obey thy Voice, and flee to Christ with Speed:
Prostrate I'll fall, and make my heavy Moan,
And wrestle humbly at his gracious Throne ;
Display my Wants, and spread my mortal Sore
Before his Face, and Mercy thus implore.
" Most gracious God, who dwell'st in peerless Ligh
" Canst Thou behold, and not abhor the Sight,
" A poor polluted Mortal ! lost ! undone !
" Roll'd in his Blood before Thy holy Throne?
" Sin is my Burden ! Sin is all my Grief !
" And Lord, to Thee I'm come to beg Relief.
" Wilt Thou not ease so deep a wounded Soul,
" Who in his Blood is forc'd to lie and roll ?

* Gen. xxxii. 29.   ‡ Luke xvi.   § Ezek. xvi. 6.

"

" Is there no *Balm in Gilead?* Lord, I'm sure,
" There's a *Physician* can effect my cure.
" Where are Thy Bowels, Lord? Is Mercy fled?
" Remember that rich blood that Jesus shed!
" If for this Plea Thou canst not ease my Grief,
" Then, Lord, I die! hopeless without Relief!
" But why didst Thou, dear Jesus, suffer? why,
" If not to take my heinous Guilt away?
" No Guile was found in Thee; no sinful Stain,
" To cause Thy Death: for me wast Thou not slain?
" Didst Thou not Justice fully satisfy?
" And pay my Debt? yet must I Prisoner lie,
" When Restitution to the full is made,
" And ev'ry Mite for my Remission paid?
" Ah! Lord, to Thee I lift my humble cry,
" Knock off these Bolts! set me at Liberty.
" See how I languish, sinking in the Mire;
" Haste, Lord, in Mercy, e'er my Soul expire!
" Why must I bleed? did I not bleed before,
" In Thy sad Wounds? Can Justice challenge more?
" My Heart-strings sure will break, I pant, I groan,
" I tremble, Lord, whilst Thou stand'st looking on!
" Dost Thou not hear the Ravens when they cry?
" And canst Thou still my humble Suit deny?
" Wilt Thou the Door of Mercy ne'er unlock?
" Lord, ope' to me, for at Thy Call I knock*,
" O *Son of David help!* for at Thy Word
" I humbly trust: Mercy to me afford."

* Matt. vii. 7.

JESUS.

Jesus.

What deep Complaint is this accosts mine Ear?
What wretched Creature's Groan is this I hear,
Who still implores my Help, and gives not o'er,
Tho' I am silent, but cries out the more?

Youth.

Lord, 'tis a wretched Sinner; lost! undone!
Seeking Salvation in Thy Name alone.

Jesus.

But know'st thou not that I was only sent,
To *Jacob*'s Race, their Ruin to prevent?
Then how darest thou who art of *Gentile* Stock,
Come boldly thus at Mercy's Door to knock?
Depart from me, and think no more to speed,
Since thou art not of *Israel*'s chosen Seed.

Youth.

Ah! gracious Lord, some kind Compassion show!
If Thou deny'st me whither shall I go?

Jesus.

But is it meet that I should take and feed
Such hungry Dogs with Children's precious Bread?

Youth.

'Tis true, O Lord; I own this Truth withal,
Yet may the Dogs lick up the Crumbs that fall
From their own Master's Board; then let a Whelp
Obtain this Favour: gracious Saviour Help!

Jesus.

Jesus.

What aileth thee, poor Soul? What's thy Complaint,
Which makes thy contrite Heart begin to faint?

Youth.

Dear Lord, Thou know'ſt my Ails: no Place is free,
But none of them, O Lord, are hid from Thee.
I am a Sinner, loathſome, vile and baſe;
I hate myſelf, and bluſh before Thy Face:
A filthy Lump of ſinful Fleſh unclean;
A viler Creature ſure has never been.
Under my dreadful Burden, lo, I faint;
Lord, look on me, and eaſe my ſad Complaint!

Jesus.

Peace, troubled Soul; I'll wipe thy briny Tears:
Great is thy Faith! thy Groans have reach'd mine Ears.
My Bowels move; nor can I more refrain
To hear thy Cries, and mitigate thy Pain.
Thy wounds affect me, and thy bitter Cry
Pierces my Heart; I feel thy Miſery.
Now what is thy Requeſt? make known to me:
What doſt thou lack? what ſhall I do for thee?
Open thy Heart to me, for I am nigh
To hear thy Suit, and all thy Wants ſupply*.

Youth.

Lord, not for worldly Wealth, nor carnal Eaſe,
Nor Honours, which th' ambitious Mind would pleaſe:
Nor Length of Days do I entreat to have,
But ſomething better, Lord, I humbly crave.

* Matt. xv. 22,——28.

'This World's a Bubble; all a Phantom vain!
There's nothing here that can aſſuage my Pain.
Such is my dreadful State, none elſe can ſave,
But Thou that call'dſt dead *Lazarus* from the Grave.
Knock off theſe Bolts, and ſet Thy Priſoner free,
O! give Thy *Spirit*, and Thy *Grace* to me.
My fainting Heart, Lord, comfort and refreſh;
Quicken my Soul, but mortify the Fleſh.
Complete the Work thou haſt in me begun;
Tho' I'm unworthy to be call'd thy Son,
Yet let me as an hired Servant be,
In any Office that belongs to thee.
'But more eſpecially, dear Lord, impart
Thy heavenly *Grace* to purify my Heart.
O! take away all my polluted Dreſs,
And cloath my Soul with Thy own Righteouſneſs.
There's nothing, Lord, I ſee will do me good,
Without a Balſam of Thy precious Blood:
My languid Soul will faint away and die,
Unleſs Thy Spirit ſpeedily apply
This ſov'reign Med'cine to my bleeding Wounds,
In which alone Salvation free abounds.
For this, dear Lord, long have I made my Moan,
With briny Tears before thy gracious Throne.
Grant my Requeſt, O Lord, and ſet me free,
For nought beſide will eaſe, or comfort me.
Make manifeſt Thy Love to my poor Soul;
O this will cure my Wounds and make me whole!
My gaſping Soul is here diſſolv'd in Tears,
While pleas'd with Hopes, and yet depreſt with Fears
But, Lord, theſe gloomy Clouds Thou canſt diſpel,
Thy Preſence makes a Heav'n, Thine Abſence Hell

All Things are possible to them that believe.

For there is nought on Earth, or Heav'n above,
Which I esteem, or value like Thy Love.
Then, Lord, some Token give; some Word apply
To my poor Heart before I droop and die.
Behold my trembling Soul in deep Distress,
Conscious, O Lord, of my unworthiness!
When I review my Sins, and Lusts so strong,
So num'rous, and persisted in so long;
How I have griev'd, and put Thy Soul to Pain;
These doleful Thoughts e'en cut my Heart in Twain.

   Thy Messengers I've slighted, and refus'd,
And my own *Conscience* grievously abus'd,
Which Thou hast given Commission from Thy Hand,
Either to clear, or sharply reprimand.
To *Truth*, alas! how deaf hath been mine Ear?
But, ah! how ready Satan's Voice to hear!
Lord, I have slighted Thee, my Sins t' embrace,
And this with Shame confounds my blushing Face.
Ah! should'st Thou yet save such a Wretch as me,
And from my Shame and Bondage set me free,
And all Thy just deserved Wrath remove,
T' embrace my Soul into Thine Arms of Love,
This will be Grace indeed, so rich, so free,
Beyond Expression! worthy, Lord, of Thee!
Now speak, dear Saviour, speak, and ease my Pain;
One gracious Smile, O let me but obtain!

JESUS.

   Chear up, poor Soul, if thou canst but believe,
And as free Gifts my Benefits receive.
Dost think that I am able to impart,
And willing too to heal thy broken Heart?

Canst thou by Faith my Promises receive?
All things are possible, couldst thou believe.

YOUTH.

Alas, my Faith is weak, O send Relief!
Lord, I believe! help Thou my unbelief!
Thy chearing Voice, that lately pierc'd mine Ear,
Again repeat, O that will slay my Fear!
If Love as well as Pity Thou wilt show,
'Twill Joy create, and banish all my Woe.
But should'st thou, Lord, my Case commiserate,
And yet thus leave me in a dying State;
As o'er *Jerus'lem* Thou did'st once lament,
Yet gave them not a Spirit to repent;
I own 'twere just, should'st Thou thus deal with me,
And leave me in my Guilt and Misery.
But should'st Thou pity this my helpless Case,
And magnify Thy rich forgiving Grace,
On such a worthless sinful Worm as me,
This would indeed surprizing Mercy be!
Speak now, dear Saviour! ease my troubled Breast!
O give my heavy laden Spirits rest!
Help, help, O Lord! my fainting Soul will die,
Unless Thou send'st with Speed a kind Reply.

JESUS.

Fear not, poor Soul, my *Grace* to thee I'll send:
My Love's Eternal, lo, it hath no End;
And this thou hast already in thy Heart;
And all Things needful I'll to thee impart.

Thy

Christ's rich and precious Promises applied. 89

Thy scarlet Sin behold I'll wash away; }
Not one of them at the great Judgment-Day }
Shall rise against thee, or thy Soul dismay. }
Now thou may'st lift thy joyful Eyes to Heav'n; }
Thy num'rous Sins, tho' great, are all forgiv'n:
For, lo, I came to seek and save the Lost,
And I am able, to the Uttermost,
To heal the Wounded, and the Needy save,
Ev'n all who can no other Helper have.
   And whoso comes to me, I'll in no wise
Reject their Suit: therefore lift up thine Eyes,
Behold, my Hands and Feet, and doubt no more,
For I have wash'd thee in my purple Gore.
Thy Debts are cancell'd with my dying Blood,
And I've repair'd the broken Law of God.
Enter the Paradise of Love unstain'd,
For, lo, thou hast the royal Fort obtain'd.
Take up thy Rest in my eternal Love;
Despise this World, thy Treasure lies above.
  Cheer up thy Heart, I tell thee thou art mine,
For with my Blood, I've bought that Soul of thine.
With endless Joys thy Heart I'll satisfy,
And in my Bosom thou shalt ever lie.
Within my circling Arms, lo, thee I take,
Now trust my Word, I'll never thee forsake *.
When thro' the *Fire* thou passest I'll be by,
And thro' the *Water* thou shalt find me nigh ‡.
Yea, I'll be with thee always to the End,
And Death at last I'll cause to be thy Friend.

     * Heb. xiii. 5.   ‡ Isa. xliii. 2.

I'll make that Passage easy, and thereby
Waft thee to my eternal Joys on high.
There thou shalt join the Army of the bless'd,
And share with them the everlasting Rest;
Where Living Water in a cryſtal Flood,
Flows out for ever from the Throne of God.
And there the Trees of Life, on either Hand,
With monthly Fruits in glorious Order ſtand*.
There ſhalt thou ſee, not darkly thro' a Glaſs,
Thy God and Saviour's Glory Face to Face.
Yea, there a King and Prieſt thou ſhalt be crown'd,
To reign with me upon a Throne renown'd †:
O'er all thy Foes thou ſhalt victorious prove,
And reſt for ever happy in my Love:
For thoſe I love, I love them to the End;
Eternity can ne'er my Fulneſs ſpend.

YOUTH.

Amazing Change! Darkneſs is fled and gone,
And lo, a glorious Day comes gliding on!
The Son of Righteouſneſs, with healing Ray,
In my Horizon now begins his Way.
My Soul is raviſh'd with the Heav'nly Light;
Loſt in ſweet Wonder, Love, and pure Delight.
My Heart is melted with celeſtial Fire,
And has obtain'd at laſt its own Deſire.
The Door is open'd; Chriſt is enter'd in,
And hath o'ercome, and ſlain the Man of Sin.
My Heart that was ſo hard is made to yield,
My heavenly Captain now has won the Field.

* Rev. xxii. 1, 2.   † Rom. v. 17.

The War is ended 'twixt my Lord and me;
And Peace is settled for Eternity.
O glorious Foretaste of eternal Bliss!
What Joy, what Pleasure can compare with this?
Great was my Burden; but, behold, my Rest
Is greater far! It cannot be exprest!
What Soul can taste of these transcendent Joys,
And not account Earth's Pleasures empty Toys!
Such sweet Effects flow from the bless'd new Birth,
Sadness is turn'd to Joy; Heav'n found on Earth.
How blind was I! senseless, bewitch'd, and mad!
I thought in Christ no Pleasure could be had.
Religion was, I thought, an empty Thing,
And neither Profit, nor Delight could bring.
Strangely I thought Professors were allur'd,
When I beheld what Suff'rings they endur'd.
But now convinc'd, I see my mad Mistake,
And I could now, thro' Grace, for Jesus Sake,
Freely with them their fiercest Storms go thro',
Such a blest Prospect lies within my View.
All Earth's Enjoyments I'd for ever slight,
For one sweet Dram of this divine Delight,
That I enjoy in my Redeemer's Love;
Which makes me long to be with him above.
Ah! that's my Home! my proper Resting-place;
My highest Hope to see him Face to Face.
Mean Time, O Lord, while here on Earth I stay,
Give me to know thy Will, and Pow'r t' obey.
Help me aloud thy Wonders to declare
Amongst thy chosen People every where;
That all may know the Riches of thy Grace,
And Sinners flock thy Gospel to embrace.

Since

Since Thou haſt rais'd me from the loweſt Pit,
And on the Rock of Ages ſet my Feet;
Fain would my Voice th' Angelic Hoſts out-vie,
And raiſe thy Praiſes far above the Sky.
O may my Heart, and Tongue, and Life make known
The wond'rous Things which Thou to me haſt ſhown;
That by thy Grace I daily may aſpire,
Nearer and nearer Thy celeſtial Choir!
Fain would I with thoſe ſwift wing'd Legions join,
To celebrate with them Thy Grace divine:
But, Lord, let Patience hold out to the End,
Nor let Corruption prompt me to offend.
O! crucify, and kill each ſinful Thought,
Let ev'ry Foe be to Submiſſion brought:
And let me ſpend the Remnant of my Days,
Wholly devoted to thy glorious Praiſe;
'Till Life's tempeſtuous Sea, Death wafts me o'er,
And lands me ſafe on *Canaan*'s heav'nly Shore.
O happy Period! then ſhall I enjoy
My Lord's dear Preſence: Bliſs without annoy.

TRUTH.

What bleſs'd triumphant Soul is this I hear;
Whoſe Voice ſounds ſo melodious in mine Ear *?
With Eagle's Wings he ſoareth up on high †,
And ſeems to aim his Flight above the Sky.
In God's eternal Love he ſeems to reſt,
Fill'd with his Grace, and of the Crown poſſeſt.
Raviſh'd with Love, and full of inward Peace,
Chearful he runs, nor faints amidſt the Race.

* Sol. Song, iv. 3.   † Iſa. xl. 31.

Yet

Yet in his higheſt Raptures can't expreſs
His deep Humility and Thankfulneſs.

YOUTH.

'Tis I, bleſt *Truth:* the Conqueſt now is won,
Grace has prevail'd, and I'm the conquer'd One.
My Grief is turn'd to Joy; and my ſad Night
Become the Day of everlaſting Light.
Great is thy Pow'r, O *Truth,* when God with thee
Attempts to gain a glorious Victory!
O'er any bold and ſtubborn Rebel Worm;
What Wonders can thy mighty Pow'r perform!
 Bleſt be the Day that thou waſt ſent to me,
To ope' mine Eyes, and ſet the Priſ'ner free.
True Love to thee for ever I'll retain,
Long as I ſhall a Pilgrim here remain:
I'll keep thee cloſe and hide thee in my Heart,
Nor for a World with thee my Jewel part.
To loſe my All on Earth, my Heart is free,
Rather than part, O precious *Truth* with thee!
Should Earth and Hell againſt my Soul engage,
And ſtir up all their Fury, Wrath, and Rage;
Lo, I thro' Grace a thouſand Deaths will die,
E'er I'll diſgrace thy Name, or thee deny.
Tho bold Deceivers, in a Multitude,
Break in upon my Soul, unlearn'd and rude,
To wreſt thy Meaning in a thouſand Forms;
Yet prompt by *Grace,* I'll ſtand their fierceſt Storms;
For by Experience I can all refute,
Who craftily againſt thee would diſpute.
Tho. ſome aſſert, thy Words but Letters are,
Empty and dead; poor, light and worthleſs Ware:
                                        But

Youth begs now the strictest Search of Truth.

But by the Spirit of my God I see
Treasures immensely rich contain'd in thee.
　Ah! did these Fools but rightly understand,
Thy pow'rful Infl'ence in the Spirit's Hand;
And could they taste thy Sweetness, they'd extol
Thy Worth above all Things from Pole to Pole.
Thy Light diffus'd in *Conscience*, I receive,
Gladly embrace, and steadfastly believe.
Highly I prize thy Beams; those chearing Rays
Sublimest Wisdom to my Soul conveys.
Thou art a glorious Gift God hath bestow'd
On Men, to guide them in the heav'nly Road;
For were it not for thy celestial Light,
Lo, we should wander in an endless Night!
And these our fav'rite Isles had surely been
As dark as others had we never seen
The Gospel Day, which round our Tents hath shone,
Whereby the great Salvation is made known.
　But now, O *Truth*, once more I come to thee,
To hear what thou wilt say concerning me:
Give in thy Verdict freely, never spare;
What e'er thou see'st amiss in me declare.
Search me and try me with a watchful Eye,
For I retain a secret Jealousy
O'er my own Heart, because I've often seen
In former Times, how I deceiv'd have been.

TRUTH.

　Conscience, to thee I must once more appeal,
Give in thy Judgment: thou caust best reveal
How Matters stand betwixt this Youth and thee;
Dost thou condemn him now, or set him free?

Cans*t*

Canst thou descry no secret Lust within?
Or doth he now discard each darling Sin?
Now let thy Verdict perfectly be giv'n,
According to thy Light receiv'd from Heav'n.

CONSCIENCE.

Truth, I am always willing at thy Word,
Judgment to give as thou dost Light afford;
And never was I willinger than now
To give in Evidence of what I know,
Concerning this young Man, O sacred *Truth*,
Lo, he is now become another *Youth*
Than what he was; *Grace* has subdu'd his Heart,
And he is truly chang'd in ev'ry Part:
Those Christian Graces in him sweetly shine,
Which plainly prove the Work to be divine.
That Faith that works by Love predominates,
And now each former sinful Course he hates.
Those very Lusts that suffer'd no Controul,
Are now become the hatred of his Soul.
Where Pride long dwelt, humility is plac'd;
Where Rage, behold, his Soul with Meekness grac'd.
Instead of Falshood, now he fears a Lie,
And most of all abhors Hypocrisy.
His *Will* and his *Affections* are set right,
And in the Law of God is his Delight.
All Christ's Commands he chearfully obeys,
Without Reserves, Excuses, or Delays.
He grieveth most for Sins that are unseen
By outward Eyes; his secret Thoughts within.
Yea he is more in Substance than in show,
When Joy runs high, his humble Heart is low.

All his own Righteoufnefs he now counts Drofs,
And what he thought his Gain he counts as Lofs.
He now abhors his former legal Drefs,
And only mentions *Jefu*'s Righteoufnefs.
Yea, Chrift is now fo precious in his Sight,
He is his only Theme of fweet Delight:
And for his Sake he freely takes the Crofs,
Nor fhuns the Scandal, nor avoids the Lofs;
But freely parts with Wealth, Good-name, and Eafe;
Nor counts Life dear, his deareft Lord to pleafe.
Earth's beft Enjoyments now he fees are vain,
Compar'd with Chrift, he treats them with Difdain.
Chrift is the only One in his Efteem,
And all his Offices are dear to him.
He alfo ufes me moft tenderly,
Becaufe from God is my Authority.
He takes my Part at all Times, nor difdains
Whate'er Reproach, or Lofs he thus fuftains.
Chrift in his Heart has fixt his regal Throne,
And other Lords he will in no wife own.
None other will he fuffer, or obey,
Chrift muft alone in him the Sceptre fway.
He'd fuffer Death before he'd flinch or yield
To let a Rival take the conquer'd Field,
Chrift's royal Property in his dear Soul:
Boldly he ftands, and fuffers no controul.
In ev'ry Thing he ftriveth to maintain
Chrift's Honour pure, without a Spot or Stain.

TRUTH.

O happy Youth! thou'rt bleffed from above;
Fill'd with the *Grace*, and ravifh'd with the *Love*

Of thy Eternal Lover, on whose Breast
Thou now lean'st on, and shalt for ever rest.
Long shall thine Honour last; thy Flowers ne'er fade:
Thy Treasure lies where Thieves can ne'er invade*.
Thy Pleasures are substantial: there's no Sting
Follows thy Mirth: from thence shall ever spring
Rivers of sweet Delight, without annoy,
Nor shall thy Tide of Bliss e'er ebb, or cloy.
Eternal Life is thine; thou shalt not die,
But conquer Death, and reign eternally †.

NEIGHBOURS.

Amazing change! no Tongue can e'er express
The inward Peace, the Joy and Happiness
This *Youth* enjoys; while by Faith's Eye he sees
How all God's Dealing answers his Decrees,
And how each Attribute at once agrees ‡.
Now *Truth* and *Conscience* with the *Spirit* meet,
And harmonize to make his Joy complete.
It now appears he's from all Bondage free,
And quite deliver'd from Captivity.
The Spirit of Adoption to him giv'n
Shews he's new-born, and made an Heir of Heav'n,
Joint Heir with Christ, in his eternal Bliss ∥:
O what amazing Happiness is this!

But while thus fill'd with Joy and sweet Delight,
Behold the *Devil* comes with all his Might;
Boldly assaults his Faith, and would destroy
If possible, his present Flood of Joy.

* Matt. vi. 20.   † John xi. 26.
‡ Psal. lxxxv. 10.   ∥ Rom. viii. 17.

Now, Satan failing in one Enterprize,
Another Project presently he tries.
But when he cann't prevail he then breaks out
To spit his hellish Venom all about,
Which in some Measure may from hence appear,
In his own Language as 'tis copy'd here.

Devil.

But hark, thou cursed Wretch! Vengeance is mine?
And I'll repay't upon that Soul of thine.
My dreadful Fury now shall fall on thee,
If thou return'st not and submit'st to me.
If all my shining Glory won't invite,
Nor all my Pow'rful Agents thee excite
To leave that Path, that cursed narrow Way;
Then I'll contrive thy Ruin, and repay
The Slights, and the Affronts I've had from thee;
And thou shalt feel how thou hast injur'd me.
Tho' from thy Heart I've been debarr'd of late,
And forc'd a little from thee to retreat;
Yet I'll return, and like a Lion strong,
Tear thy whole Soul to Pieces e'er't be long.

Youth.

Father of Lies, dost think I dread thy Frown?
'Tis past thy Pow'r or Skill to cast me down.
Thy Head is bruis'd: thou art a conquer'd Foe;
And chain'd up fast; no further can'st thou go
Than thou art suffer'd by my God and King;
Therefore I fear not; thou hast lost thy Sting.
Since Christ himself is on my Side engag'd,
I'm not dismay'd, howe'er thou art enrag'd

Against

Against my Soul; for all the Pow'rs of Heav'n
If needful, would be for my Safeguard giv'n;
And would protect me from the Pow'rs of Hell,
Howe'er the Billows of that Lake might swell.
Therefore be gone, vile Tempter; hence depart;
Go! like a roaring Lion as thou art,
Walking about, and seeking to devour
Each precious Soul that falls within thy Pow'r.
But all thy Stratagems abortive prov'd
Against my Lord, and all his dear Belov'd:
For all whom his eternal Love hath chose,
His pow'rful Arms eternally inclose.
And thus by Faith, behold, I firmly stand,
Safely surrounded by my Saviour's Hand.

DEVIL.

Ah! self-conceited Soul, dost thou believe
That God will all thy youthful Crimes forgive?
And that thou shalt be able still to stand
Strictly obedient to his stern Command?
No I'll convince thee of this Falsity;
The Lord will soon become thine Enemy,
Altho' thou think'st he's now become thy Friend,
A small Temptation will make thee Offend
Against his harsh Commands; then will he fly,
And in his Wrath forsake thee utterly:
Then will I rent and tear thee as I list,
And thou shalt find no Pow'r will thee assist.

YOUTH.

Thou boasting baffled Foe, thy Threats give o'er,
For I am rescu'd from thy Wiles and Pow'r.

God hath on me beſtow'd his ſpecial *Grace*,
And I abhor thy Ways, nor will give Place
To thee, O Satan! therefore hence depart,
For thou a flatt'ring falſe Deceiver art.
And tho' thou ſtriveſt daily to entice,
And draw me in to be a Slave to Vice,
As too too long I've been; yet God hath ſaid,
" My *Grace* ſhall be ſufficient for thine Aid."
Therefore I'm ſatisfy'd thou ne'er ſhalt be
Able by any Means to conquer me.
And if thro' Weakneſs I were overcome,
God would not then pronounce in Wrath my Doom.
Chriſt is my Advocate; he pleads my Cauſe,
And hath repair'd his Father's broken Laws.
Therefore though God chaſtiſe, he'll not remove
From me his tender, and eternal Love *.

DEVIL.

Thy Hopes will fail, and ſoon black Clouds will hide
Thy blazing Sun; thy Steps will quickly ſlide:
Thy Morning bright will ſoon be overcaſt,
And all thy Joys will but a Moment laſt.
And what though *Truth* and *Conſcience* both agree,
Soon will th' old Proverb be made good in thee,
That the young Saint will an old Devil prove,
And bitter Enmity ſucceed thy Love;
So that at laſt in black Apoſtaſy
Thou wilt a bold ſtout-hearted Rebel die.

YOUTH.

Ah! *Satan*, ſince thou'ſt loſt thy bleſs'd Eſtate,
Man's Happineſs thou look'ſt on with Regret;

Therefore

* Pſal. lxxxix. 32, 33.

Therefore againſt my Soul thou ſhews thy Spite,
But, lo, thy Teeth are broke, thou canſt not bite:
Becauſe thou haſt for ever loſt thy Crown,
At me thou caſteſt forth an envious Frown :
And ſince thou waſt a Morning Star of Light,
And now art ſunk into eternal Night;
Therefore thou ſtriveſt daily to betray,
And draw my Feet to thy pernicious Way.
But all thy crafty Stratagems are vain,
Thy helliſh Purpoſe thou canſt ne'er obtain.
No Pow'r can break that bleſſed Unity,
Which is conjoin'd betwixt my Lord and me.
I'm fix'd in him ; my Standing ſure is made ;
None can my bright eternal Crown invade.
He that hath in my Soul this Work begun,
Will never leave it off 'till he has done.
There's not a Sheep nor Lamb in all his Fold,
But his ſtrong Arm eternally ſhall hold.
And in the greateſt Danger they ſhall ſtand,
None can them pluck from his Almighty Hand *.
In ev'ry Nation by his Pow'r they're kept,
Till from all Dangers they are clean eſcapt,
And landed ſafely on the heav'nly Shore,
Where Sin and Sorrow ſhall be known no more.
Thus on the Rock of Ages am I plac'd,
And my Foundation ne'er can be eras'd.
Tho' Mountains ſhould depart and Hills remove,
Chriſt cannot change his everlaſting Love ;
Or let his endleſs Covenant of Peace
Be e'er remov'd, or his rich Mercy ceaſe.

* John x. 28, 29.

And now since *Truth* and *Conscience* both agree,
To prove a saving Change is wrought in me,
Th' immortal Seed is sown, and not in vain;
It cannot fail to bring immortal Grain,
Which must and shall eternally remain.
For whom God calls, he also justifies,
And not one of them an Apostate dies*.

* The Doctrine of the final Perseverance of the Saints, being here asserted in the strongest Terms, in answer to the hellish Suggestion of Satan going before; which I think could not be fully answered, without such bold Assertions gathered from the Word of God, which is the Sword of the Spirit; yet lest it should be abused by any bold Presumers, the following Caution is here offered to every such Reader, viz. Remember that he who said, "All that the Father "giveth me, shall come unto me; and he that cometh unto "me, I will in no wise cast out." And, "If any Man eat "of this Bread, he shall live for ever." Hath also said, "If "a man abide not in me, he is cast forth as a Branch, and is "withered, and Men gather them, and cast them into the "Fire, and they are burned." Again, "If ye keep my "Commandments, ye shall abide in my Love; even as I "have kept my Father's Commandments, and abide in his "Love." *John* vi. 37, 51. xv. 6, 10. And by the same Authority speaks an inspired Apostle, "Let him that thinketh "he standeth, take heed lest he fall." Again, speaking concerning the breaking off of the *Jews*, "Thou wilt say then, the "Branches were broken off, that I might be graffed in. Well, "because of Unbelief they were broken off, and thou stand- "est by Faith. Be not high-minded, but fear. For if God "spared not the natural Branches, take Heed lest he also spare "not thee. Behold therefore the Goodness and Severity of "God: on them which fell, Severity; but towards thee, "Goodness; if thou continue in his Goodness: Otherwise "thou also shalt be cut off; 1 *Cor.* x. 12. *Rom.* xi. 19, 20, "21, 22."

Members of Chrift's own Body, lo, they are,
And Head and Members all one Nature fhare :
Therefore as lives the Head, e'en fo fhall I,
And reign with him to all Eternity.

Devil.

I fee my Words no Place at all can find
Within the Circle of thy headftrong Mind:
Therefore I'll leave thee with my dreadful Curfe,
Which is as bad as Hell; yea it is worfe.
Than all the Plagues of Hell's fictitious Lake,
Which now thou dread'ft; and let my Agents take
Vengeance upon that curfed Soul of thine
'Till thou thy hateful Purpofes decline.
And tho' at prefent I depart, yet lo,
I'll come again within a Day or two,
And will thy Soul fo grievoufly torment,
That thou of thy Repentance fhalt repent.

Youth.

Away, foul Fiend! Bleft be the glorious Pow'r
That hath preferv'd me in this needful Hour,
When fo affaulted by that cruel Foe,
Whofe Grand Defign is my fole Overthrow.
Lord in thy Strength I've fought, and made him flee,
Therefore all Thanks, Glory and Praife to thee.
Now with celeftial Fire my Soul inflame,
And teach me, Lord, to magnify thy Name :
And if again the Tempter fhould come near,
O let thy *Truth* in my Behalf appear!
Then in thy Srength, tho' young and weak, fhall I
O'ercome th' Affaults of ev'ry Enemy.

Speak

Speak now, O *Truth*, wilt thou be on my Side,
For in thy Help I mightily confide?
Tho' I am weak, yet if thy mighty Pow'r,
Be on my Side, none can my Soul devour.

TRUTH.

Yes, I'll assist thee, *Youth*, with all my Might,
Against thy Foes, the Sons of Hell and Night.
I'll with my pow'rful Sword cut down and slay
All those curst Fiends that dare beset thy Way *.
Depend on me, I'll clearly light thy Path
Thro' this frail Life, and thro' the Vale of Death †.

GRACE.

I'll second *Truth*, and all thy Wants supply,
Fear not, nor doubt of my Sufficiency ‡.
I'll be thy Light in Darkness, Joy in Grief;
Yea, and in all thy Troubles bring Relief.
Only believe, and on my Aid rely,
Thy Foes with Shame shall all be forc'd to fly.
Never did any on my Strength depend,
But they obtain'd Salvation in the End.
Then trust me, *Youth*, whene'er thou art distrest;
I'll bring thee safe to thine eternal Rest.

CONSCIENCE.

I'll be the third to lend an helping Hand,
With *Grace* and *Truth*, we'll make a triple Band.
A threefold Cord cannot be quickly broke,
As *Truth* hath for thy solid Comfort spoke §.

* Eph. vi. 17. † Ps. cxix. 105. ‡ 2 Cor. xii. 9. § Eccl. iv. 12.

Conscience *concludes the definitive Treaty.*

Then Foes from Earth or Hell thou need'ſt not fear,
For I thy faithful Witneſs ſtill am near,
While thus thou walk'ſt in Truth before the Lord,
And all thy Ways are order'd by his Word.
   Satan, confounded, ſhall be put to flight,
And thy pure Candle daily ſhine more bright:
Nor can the Fiend e'ermore recover Ground,
While thus I teſtify thy Heart is found.
Then chear up, *Youth,* and bid adieu to Woe,
Nor fear th' Aſſaults of thy accuſing Foe;
For to thy Maſter thee I'll recommend,
And be thy faithful Witneſs to the End.
And my beſt Cordials I'll to thee impart,
When Death's dire Shafts ſhall penetrate thy Heart.
   God's Word has been thy Rule in ev'ry Thing,
His Glory thy main Aim; his Love the Spring
Of all that Comfort, Joy, and ſweet Delight
Thou findeſt in his Favour Day and Night:
Therefore his Spirit alſo teſtifies
Thou art an Heir of Bliſs above the Skies.
Be thankful then, for thou art ſafe and bleſs'd,
Chriſt hath enſur'd thine everlaſting Reſt.

HYMNS, *and*

The YOUNG MAN *having obtained Assurance of God's Love, Peace of Conscience, and Joy in the Holy Ghost; being delivered from the Power of the Tempter; now breaks out in the following Hymns of Praise and Thanksgiving to God.*

HYMN I.

A mystical Song of Thanksgiving to God.

I.

MY Soul mounts up with Eagle's Wings,
And, Lord, to thee her God she sings,
 Since thou art reconcil'd:
Mine Enemies are forc'd to flee,
Soon as thy mighty Pow'r they see,
 For I'm become thy Child.

II.

Thou makest rich by making poor,
By emptying me thou fill'st my Store,
 Which none can do beside:
By killing, Lord, thou makest whole,
By wounding thou hast cur'd my Soul;
 Thy Name be magnify'd.

III.

Thou makest blind by giving Sight,
And turn'st the Darkness into Light,
 By Sov'reign Grace divine:
Thou cloath'st the Soul by making bare,
Thou givest Food when none is there,
 And be the Glory thine.

Thou

IV.

Thou raiseſt up by pulling down,
By humbling raiseſt to a Crown,
    Such are thy wond'rous Ways!
Thou mak'ſt the bitt'reſt Potion sweet;
Thy heavy Croſs makes Joy complete,
    And thine ſhall be the Praiſe.

V.

The conquer'd, lo, the Conqueſt gains,
The feeble Soul the Field obtains,
    By Might and Majeſty:
And this, Lord, thou haſt done for me,
All Praiſe and Glory be to thee,
    Thy Name I'll magnify.

VI.

To make Men wiſe thou mak'ſt 'em Fools,
By emptying them thou fill'ſt their Souls
    With Graces rich and free:
By making weary thou giv'ſt Reſt,
And what ſeem'd worſt, prov'd for the beſt;
    All Glory be to thee.

VII.

Thou art afar, yet always near;
Immoveable, yet ev'ry where;
    Eternally the ſame:
Thy Nature's Light, thy Nature's Love;
Thou dwell'ſt below, thou dwell'ſt above;
    All glorious is thy Name.

VIII.

Thou art a glorious Myſtery,
In Eſſence One, in Perſons Three,
    Eternal and divine:

By Saints and Angels high ador'd,
The only true and righteous Lord,
   All Praise and Glory's thine.

HYMN II.

Peace of Conscience.

I.

CONSCIENCE is now become my Friend,
  And brings sweet Messages to me:
Therefore I'll to his Words attend,
Howe'er I here reproach'd may be.
   It matters not how Men revile,
   If *God* and *Conscience* on me smile.

II.

Now I am bles'd with inward Peace,
My Chains are broke, my Soul's set free;
O how shall I adore his Grace,
Who from my Bondage ransom'd me!
   All Thanks to his Almighty Hand,
   Who paid the Law its full Demand.

III.

Now *Conscience* brings me precious Food,
Sent from the King of Kings on high:
My Dainties are so rich and good,
Fully my Soul they satisfy:
   Their worth can never be declar'd,
   Nor ought on Earth therewith compar'd.

IV.

When *Conscience* first became my Friend,
I was o'erwhelm'd with Seas of Grief:

                         Then

Then did the Lord in Mercy fend
By him a Word of sweet Relief.
   Soon did the roaring Billows cease,
   And I was blest with inward Peace.
V.
Though oft I suffer'd for his Sake,
Yet O how sweet these Sufferings are!
For he my friendly Part to take,
Speaks inward Peace beyond compare.
   For if the Earth should change its Place,
   Still I am bless'd with inward Peace.
VI.
When Tempests rise and Billows roar,
And others know not where to flee:
Trembling they long to see the Shore,
But here's a joyful Calm in me,
   In secret chambers lockt up fast,
   I lie 'till all the Storms are past.
VII.
At Death, and at the Judgment-Day,
What would men give for such a Friend?
Then all who *Conscience* disobey,
Must rue their Folly without End:
   When such are forc'd to howl and cry,
   My Soul shall joyful mount on high.

HYMN III.

Joy in the Holy Ghost, Rom. viii. 15, 16.

I.

HE's come! the *Comforter* is come!
   Arise my Soul and sing:

O let thy Voice no more be dumb,
    To praise thy God and King!

II.

Let Worldlings at my Joys repine,
    And spread their Lies abroad
God's Spirit witnesses with mine,
    That I am born of God.

III.

O, this is Heav'n on Earth begun,
    And Glory in the Bud!
I taste those living Streams that run
    Out of the Throne of God.

IV.

How far does this my heav'nly Joy
    All earthly Joys exceed!
This is pure Gold without Alloy,
    From Dross and Mixture freed.

V.

Thanks to my loving Saviour's Name,
    That hung upon the Tree;
And bore my Hell, my Sin, my Shame,
    To purchase Heav'n for me.

VI.

Of this I have a transient Taste,
    But quickly shall I prove
The Sweetness of his Marriage Feast,
    Amongst his Hosts above.

VII.

There shall I feast and never tire,
    Nor shall the Pleasures cloy:
There shall I have my full Desire
    Of everlasting Joy.

HYMN IV.

Increase of Grace, and Perseverance. Heb. vi. 1, 2.

I.

REpentance in my Soul is wrought,
    And Faith is giv'n me to believe
That I had fold myself for Nought,
    But Jesus did my Soul retrieve.

II.

From Heav'n's high Court his Eye beheld,
    And down to Hell he stoop'd for me;
Ev'n while against him I rebell'd,
    He bore the Curse to set me free.

III.

Him for my *Prophet*, he alone,
    I take to teach, and guide my Way;
My *Priest*, who only can atone;
    My *King*, whom gladly I obey.

IV.

Thus am I brought to Jesu's Feet,
    With chearful Heart, and willing Hands:
To all his Ordinances sweet,
    My chearful Soul obedient stands,

V.

His Baptism, and his Supper-Feast,
    Tho' some account but carnal Things;
Yet at those Seasons, lo, I taste
    Substantial Food, and heav'nly Springs.

VI.

My dearest Lord I must obey,
    Though Men reproach me and revile:

How can I from his Precepts stray?
    Or how my Feet, new wash'd defile?

VII.
Let Men deride for Jesu's Sake,
    Yet by his Grace resolv'd am I
To follow him; his Cross to take,
    Yea, and for him submit to die.

VIII.
Nor will I ever turn my Back,
    While he inspires me with his Love;
And this I trust I ne'er shall lack,
    'Till he transports me safe above.

IX.
For this I have his Promise sure:
    In all my Straits he'll bear me through:
Therefore with Patience I endure,
    I in his Strength can all Things do.

X.
Let Satan rage, and Men conspire,
    To frustrate all my Hopes divine;
Their Plots shall fail; their Strength expire,
    God will fulfil his kind Design.

XI.
Though Death must on my Body seize,
    And Worms devour my mortal Clay:
His sov'reign Hand my Flesh shall raise
    Perfect at the great Judgment Day.

XII.
When he shall pass the final Doom
    Of Wrath, on all his stubborn Foes:
Then shall I forth triumphant come,
    With all the Children he hath chose.

XIII.

Then all his Saints moſt joyfully,
    With tender Bowels he'll embrace:
And glorious Crowns of Dignity,
    On ev'ry Head his Hand will place.

XIV.

There with his bleſs'd redeemed Throng,
    I to his Kingdom ſhall aſcend;
And there with Joy and endleſs Song,
    A bleſs'd Eternity ſhall ſpend.

HYMN V.

The Sun of Righteouſneſs. From Mal. iv. 2.

I.

BEHOLD, the Sun of Righteouſneſs
    Breaks forth with healing Beams on me!
And from my Darkneſs and Diſtreſs,
Lo, he hath ſet the Priſ'ner free!
    For I was bound in Death aud Sin,
    'Till he with quick'ning Rays broke in.

II.

How I my former Life compar'd
To the bright Seaſon of the Spring *;
For carnal Mirth I never ſpar'd,
But freely gave myſelf the Swing.
    Then was I blind; but now I ſee;
    No Light nor Life was then in me.

* See Youth's firſt Speech in the Book.

III.

My Spring was then a Winter's Sun,
As in December dark and cold;
His Light from my Horizon gone,
Nor could I then his Rays behold.
    My Heart was frozen like a Stone;
    My Leaves were off, my Sap was gone.

IV.

The Lord is now my Sun and Shield,
The Glory of the World is he:
True Light and Life his Presence yield,
And thus hath he enlighten'd me.
    His Beams such Radiency display,
    Increasing like the dawning Day.

V.

Gladly we see the nat'ral Sun,
Early salute our op'ning Eyes;
Damp Vapours his bright Presence shun;
Sweetly he clears the cloudy Skies:
    The Birds their chearful Notes begin,
    And Day with Joy they usher in.

VI.

Thus doth the Sun of Righteousness,
By his divine refulgent Rays,
Quicken my Soul when in Distress,
And fills my Heart with Joy and Praise.
    When Clouds appear, and Storms arise,
    His Presence clears the dusky Skies.

VII.

Just as the Flow'rs hang down their Head,
Lifeless till Nature them revive;

SPIRITUAL SONGS. 115

So I in Sin lay cold and dead,
'Till Chrift's bright Beams made me alive.
   My Heart in Guilt lay bury'd deep,
   'Till Chrift awoke me from my Sleep.

VIII.

O! how his Voice my Spirits chear'd,
When he fhone in upon my Heart;
Then Light and Life in me appear'd,
And I reviv'd in ev'ry Part.
   My feeble Limbs benumb'd grew ftrong,
   And Songs of Praife employ'd my Tongue.

IX.

Then, O thou Sun of Righteoufnefs!
Never withdraw Thy Rays divine;
But on my quicken'd Soul imprefs
The Image of that Soul of Thine:
   Not like the Moon that guides the Night,
   But like the Sun divinely bright.

X.

For as the radiant Sun excels
The feeble Moon and Stars of Light;
E'en fo the Soul where Jefus dwells
Excels the Sons of Nature's Night:
   Or as the Gofpel doth the Law,
   And *Sinai's* Flames which *Ifrael* faw.

XI.

But nat'ral Men defpife this Light;
And rather chufe a legal Guide;
This glorious Gofpel Sun they flight,
And all its quick'ning Pow'r deride:
   And all who walk by Wifdom's Rules,
   By them are counted worfe than Fools.

Pity

XII.

Pity thofe wretched Sons of Night,
Great Source of Light and Life divine!
Arife, and make thy Glories bright,
Through ev'ry Nation fweetly fhine.
    Open Men's blind deluded Eyes,
    That they Thy Gofpel Light may prize.

HYMN VI.

The divine Breathings of an Heaven-born Soul.

I.

LET not the Sun eclipfed be,
  Nor Clouds of Darknefs interpofe,
Betwixt Thyfelf, dear Lord, and me,
Thou ever blefied *Sharon's Rofe*.
    O let Thy Face upon me fhine,
    Since by Election I am Thine!

II.

Lord let me ftill enjoy Thy Light,
'Till Grace fhall me with Glory crown,
Turn not my Morning into Night,
Nor let my glorious Sun go down!
    O let Thy Face upon me fhine,
    Since by dear Purchafe I am Thine!

III.

Let no Corruption Clouds arife
From this dark Lump of carnal Earth,
To veil from me thofe glorious Skies,
Whence I derive my heav'nly Birth.
    O let Thy Face upon me fhine,
    For by Adoption I am Thine!

IV.

Lord make my Morning Dawn more bright,
And haften on the perfect Day :
Endue mine Eyes with ftronger Light,
To guide me in Thy heav'nly Way.
    O let Thy Face upon me fhine,
    Since God by Gift has made me Thine.

V.

O glorious Sun of Righteoufnefs,
Whofe Pow'r made this my Heart of Stone
Sufceptive of thy Seal's imprefs,
And fit for Thine eternal Throne.
    O let Thy Face upon me fhine,
    Since by fweet Contract I am Thine.

VI.

The Light of Thy dear Countenance
Is, Lord, the only Thing I prize:
Then let not clouds of Sin or Senfe
Eclipfe Thy Glory from mine Eyes.
    O let Thy Face upon me fhine,
    For I by Faith am wholly Thine.

VII.

Be Thou my Strength, my Light, my Guide ;
In ev'ry Strait for ever nigh :
From Thy dear Path ne'er let me flide,
But lead and guide me with Thine Eye.
    O let Thy Face upon me fhine,
    For I to Thee myfelf refign.

VIII.

There's many now who daily cry,
" O who will fhew us any good ?"
    Lord,

Lord in thyself all Treasures lie,
Though this by few is understood.
 Oh let Thy Face upon me shine,
  For, Lord, by Conquest I am Thine.

IX.

Lord, while Thy Presence I enjoy,
And with Thy Saints Communion have;
My Faith stands firm; Hell cann't annoy
The happy Soul Thou deign'st to save.
 O let Thy Face upon me shine,
  For I can say, "Lord, Thou art mine."

PART II.

INTERCESSION.

I.

DEAR Saviour, Sun of Righteousness,
 Not only shine on my poor Heart;
But thro' this World's wide Wilderness,
Thy healing Influence, impart.
 O let Thy Face upon them shine,
  For by Creation all are thine.

II.

Let Light and Knowledge, Lord abound,
And Thy bless'd Gospel far be spread:
And whoso would Thy Truth confound,
Let them by it be Converts made.
 O let Thy Face on *Zion* shine,
  And bless that holy Hill of Thine.

III.

Let Thy bright Glory so break forth,
And Darkness fly from ev'ry Land,

That all the Saints throughout the Earth
May in Thy Truth rejoicing stand.
   O let Thy Face upon them shine,
     Who by Election, Lord, are Thine!

IV.

Let ev'ry Nation far and near,
Thy pure unspotted Light behold:
From ev'ry Error purge them clear;
And Thy rich Gospel-Grace unfold.
   O let Thy Face upon them shine,
     For all the Nations, Lord, are Thine!

V.

Let all who bear the Christian-Name,
Thy Holy Spirit, Lord, receive;
Nor let Thine Enemies blaspheme
The heav'nly Truths that we believe.
   O let Thy Face upon them shine,
     And on them set Thy Seal Divine.

VI.

Lord carry on thy glorious Work,
Victoriously in ev'ry Land;
Let *Tartar*, *Pagan*, *Jew*, and *Turk*,
Submit themselves to Thy Command.
   O let Thy Face upon them shine,
     And gather these Out-casts of Thine!

VII.

Thy Light and Truth, O Lord, send forth,
Perspicuously thro' ev'ry Land;
That all from *East*, *South*, *West* and *North*,
May humbly bow to Thy Command.
   O let Thy Face upon them shine,
     That all may own Thy Pow'r divine!

VIII.

Set up Thy King on *Zion*'s Hill,
Upon his Father *David*'s Throne:
Thine Ancient Promises fulfil,
Made to Thine own eternal Son.
 O let Thy Face for ever shine
 Upon his Seed, Thy chosen Line!

IX.

Remember *Abr'am*, Lord, Thy Friend,
And pity *Jacob*'s chosen Race:
Open their Eyes; Thy Spirit send
And let them taste Thy promis'd Grace.
 O let Thy Face in Mercy shine
 Upon that ancient Flock of Thine!

X.

Give now the Kingdom to Thy Son,
O'er all the Globe, his Trophies spread:
Let *Jews* and *Gentiles* all in One,
Be brought to him their living Head.
 O let thy Face upon them shine,
 For *Jews* and *Gentiles* all are Thine!

XI.

Thus all the Praise shall be to Thee,
Great Parent of the Universe;
Whose Mercy sets the Pris'ner free,
Whose Light the darkest Clouds disperse:
 For Heav'n and Earth shall both combine,
 And shout, "All Glory, Lord, is Thine.

FINIS.

www.ingramcontent.com/pod-product-compliance
Lightning Source LLC
Chambersburg PA
CBHW021941160426
43195CB00011B/1175